The Poetry of Algernon Charles Swinburne

VOLUME XVII - A CHANNEL PASSAGE AND OTHER POEMS

Algernon Charles Swinburne was born on April 5th, 1837, in London, into a wealthy Northumbrian family. He was educated at Eton and at Balliol College, Oxford, but did not complete a degree.

In 1860 Swinburne published two verse dramas but achieved his first literary success in 1865 with Atalanta in Calydon, written in the form of classical Greek tragedy. The following year "Poems and Ballads" brought him instant notoriety. He was now identified with "indecent" themes and the precept of art for art's sake.

Although he produced much after this success in general his popularity and critical reputation declined. The most important qualities of Swinburne's work are an intense lyricism, his intricately extended and evocative imagery, metrical virtuosity, rich use of assonance and alliteration, and bold, complex rhythms.

Swinburne's physical appearance was small, frail, and plagued by several other oddities of physique and temperament. Throughout the 1860s and 1870s he drank excessively and was prone to accidents that often left him bruised, bloody, or unconscious. Until his forties he suffered intermittent physical collapses that necessitated removal to his parents' home while he recovered.

Throughout his career Swinburne also published literary criticism of great worth. His deep knowledge of world literatures contributed to a critical style rich in quotation, allusion, and comparison. He is particularly noted for discerning studies of Elizabethan dramatists and of many English and French poets and novelists. As well he was a noted essayist and wrote two novels.

In 1879, Swinburne's friend and literary agent, Theodore Watts-Dunton, intervened during a time when Swinburne was dangerously ill. Watts-Dunton isolated Swinburne at a suburban home in Putney and gradually weaned him from alcohol, former companions and many other habits as well.

Much of his poetry in this period may be inferior but some individual poems are exceptional; "By the North Sea," "Evening on the Broads," "A Nympholept," "The Lake of Gaube," and "Neap-Tide."

Swinburne lived another thirty years with Watts-Dunton. He denied Swinburne's friends access to him, controlled the poet's money, and restricted his activities. It is often quoted that 'he saved the man but killed the poet'.

Swinburne died on April 10th, 1909 at the age of seventy-two.

Index of Contents

A CHANNEL PASSAGE AND OTHER POEMS

IN MEMORY OF WILLIAM MORRIS AND EDWARD BURNE JONES

A CHANNEL PASSAGE

1855

Forth from Calais, at dawn of night, when sunset summer on autumn shone,
Fared the steamer alert and loud through seas whence only the sun was gone:
Soft and sweet as the sky they smiled, and bade man welcome: a dim sweet hour
Gleamed and whispered in wind and sea, and heaven was fair as a field in flower.
Stars fulfilled the desire of the darkling world as with music: the starbright air
Made the face of the sea, if aught may make the face of the sea, more fair.

Whence came change? Was the sweet night weary of rest? What anguish awoke in the dark?
Sudden, sublime, the strong storm spake: we heard the thunders as hounds that bark.
Lovelier if aught may be lovelier than stars, we saw the lightnings exalt the sky,
Living and lustrous and rapturous as love that is born but to quicken and lighten and die.
Heaven's own heart at its highest of delight found utterance in music and semblance in fire:
Thunder on thunder exulted, rejoicing to live and to satiate the night's desire.

And the night was alive and anhungered of life as a tiger from toils cast free:
And a rapture of rage made joyous the spirit and strength of the soul of the sea.
All the weight of the wind bore down on it, freighted with death for fraught:
And the keen waves kindled and quickened as things transfigured or things distraught.
And madness fell on them laughing and leaping; and madness came on the wind:
And the might and the light and the darkness of storm were as storm in the heart of Ind.
Such glory, such terror, such passion, as lighten and harrow the far fierce East,
Rang, shone, spake, shuddered around us: the night was an altar with death for priest.
The channel that sunders England from shores where never was man born free
Was clothed with the likeness and thrilled with the strength and the wrath of a tropic sea.
As a wild steed ramps in rebellion, and rears till it swerves from a backward fall,
The strong ship struggled and reared, and her deck was upright as a sheer cliff's wall.
Stern and prow plunged under, alternate: a glimpse, a recoil, a breath,

And she sprang as the life in a god made man would spring at the throat of death.
Three glad hours, and it seemed not an hour of supreme and supernal joy,
Filled full with delight that revives in remembrance a sea-bird's heart in a boy.
For the central crest of the night was cloud that thundered and flamed, sublime
As the splendour and song of the soul everlasting that quickens the pulse of time.
The glory beholden of man in a vision, the music of light overheard,
The rapture and radiance of battle, the life that abides in the fire of a word,
In the midmost heaven enkindled, was manifest far on the face of the sea,
And the rage in the roar of the voice of the waters was heard but when heaven breathed free.
Far eastward, clear of the covering of cloud, the sky laughed out into light
From the rims of the storm to the sea's dark edge with flames that were flowerlike and white.
The leaping and luminous blossoms of live sheet lightning that laugh as they fade
From the cloud's black base to the black wave's brim rejoiced in the light they made.
Far westward, throned in a silent sky, where life was in lustrous tune,
Shone, sweeter and surer than morning or evening, the steadfast smile of the moon.
The limitless heaven that enshrined them was lovelier than dreams may behold, and deep
As life or as death, revealed and transfigured, may shine on the soul through sleep.
All glories of toil and of triumph and passion and pride that it yearns to know
Bore witness there to the soul of its likeness and kinship, above and below.
The joys of the lightnings, the songs of the thunders, the strong sea's labour and rage,
Were tokens and signs of the war that is life and is joy for the soul to wage.
No thought strikes deeper or higher than the heights and the depths that the night made bare,
Illimitable, infinite, awful and joyful, alive in the summit of air—
Air stilled and thrilled by the tempest that thundered between its reign and the sea's,
Rebellious, rapturous, and transient as faith or as terror that bows men's knees.
No love sees loftier and fairer the form of its godlike vision in dreams
Than the world shone then, when the sky and the sea were as love for a breath's length seems—
One utterly, mingled and mastering and mastered and laughing with love that subsides
As the glad mad night sank panting and satiate with storm, and released the tides.
In the dense mid channel the steam-souled ship hung hovering, assailed and withheld
As a soul born royal, if life or if death be against it, is thwarted and quelled.
As the glories of myriads of glowworms in lustrous grass on a boundless lawn
Were the glories of flames phosphoric that made of the water a light like dawn.
A thousand Phosphors, a thousand Hespers, awoke in the churning sea,
And the swift soft hiss of them living and dying was clear as a tune could be;
As a tune that is played by the fingers of death on the keys of life or of sleep,
Audible alway alive in the storm, too fleet for a dream to keep: Too fleet, too sweet for a dream to recover and thought to remember awake:
Light subtler and swifter than lightning, that whispers and laughs in the live storm's wake,
In the wild bright wake of the storm, in the dense loud heart of the labouring hour,
A harvest of stars by the storm's hand reaped, each fair as a star-shaped flower.
And sudden and soft as the passing of sleep is the passing of tempest seemed
When the light and the sound of it sank, and the glory was gone as a dream half dreamed.
The glory, the terror, the passion that made of the midnight a miracle, died,
Not slain at a stroke, nor in gradual reluctance abated of power and of pride;
With strong swift subsidence, awful as power that is wearied of power upon earth,
As a God that were wearied of power upon heaven, and were fain of a new God's birth,
The might of the night subsided: the tyranny kindled in darkness fell:

And the sea and the sky put off them the rapture and radiance of heaven and of hell.
The waters, heaving and hungering at heart, made way, and were well-nigh fain,
For the ship that had fought them, and wrestled, and revelled in labour, to cease from her pain.
And an end was made of it: only remembrance endures of the glad loud strife;
And the sense that a rapture so royal may come not again in the passage of life.

THE LAKE OF GAUBE

The sun is lord and god, sublime, serene,
And sovereign on the mountains: earth and air
Lie prone in passion, blind with bliss unseen
By force of sight and might of rapture, fair
As dreams that die and know not what they were.
The lawns, the gorges, and the peaks, are one
Glad glory, thrilled with sense of unison
In strong compulsive silence of the sun.

Flowers dense and keen as midnight stars aflame
And living things of light like flames in flower
That glance and flash as though no hand might tame
Lightnings whose life outshone their stormlit hour
And played and laughed on earth, with all their power
Gone, and with all their joy of life made long
And harmless as the lightning life of song,
Shine sweet like stars when darkness feels them strong.

The deep mild purple flaked with moonbright gold
That makes the scales seem flowers of hardened light,
The flamelike tongue, the feet that noon leaves cold,
The kindly trust in man, when once the sight
Grew less than strange, and faith bade fear take flight,
Outlive the little harmless life that shone
And gladdened eyes that loved it, and was gone
Ere love might fear that fear had looked thereon.

Fear held the bright thing hateful, even as fear,
Whose name is one with hate and horror, saith
That heaven, the dark deep heaven of water near,
Is deadly deep as hell and dark as death.
The rapturous plunge that quickens blood and breath
With pause more sweet than passion, ere they strive
To raise again the limbs that yet would dive
Deeper, should there have slain the soul alive.

As the bright salamander in fire of the noonshine exults and is glad of his day,
The spirit that quickens my body rejoices to pass from the sunlight away,

To pass from the glow of the mountainous flowerage, the high multitudinous bloom,
Far down through the fathomless night of the water, the gladness of silence and gloom.
Death-dark and delicious as death in the dream of a lover and dreamer may be,
It clasps and encompasses body and soul with delight to be living and free:
Free utterly now, though the freedom endure but the space of a perilous breath,
And living, though girdled about with the darkness and coldness and strangeness of death:
Each limb and each pulse of the body rejoicing, each nerve of the spirit at rest,
All sense of the soul's life rapture, a passionate peace in its blindness blest.
So plunges the downward swimmer, embraced of the water unfathomed of man,
The darkness unplummeted, icier than seas in midwinter, for blessing or ban;
And swiftly and sweetly, when strength and breath fall short, and the dive is done,
Shoots up as a shaft from the dark depth shot, sped straight into sight of the sun;
And sheer through the snow-soft water, more dark than the roof of the pines above,
Strikes forth, and is glad as a bird whose flight is impelled and sustained of love.
As a sea-mew's love of the sea-wind breasted and ridden for rapture's sake
Is the love of his body and soul for the darkling delight of the soundless lake:
As the silent speed of a dream too living to live for a thought's space more
Is the flight of his limbs through the still strong chill of the darkness from shore to shore.
Might life be as this is and death be as life that casts off time as a robe,
The likeness of infinite heaven were a symbol revealed of the lake of Gaube.

Whose thought has fathomed and measured
The darkness of life and of death,
The secret within them treasured,
The spirit that is not breath?
Whose vision has yet beholden
The splendour of death and of life?
Though sunset as dawn be golden,
Is the word of them peace, not strife?
Deep silence answers: the glory
We dream of may be but a dream,
And the sun of the soul wax hoary
As ashes that show not a gleam.
But well shall it be with us ever
Who drive through the darkness here,
If the soul that we live by never,
For aught that a lie saith, fear.

THE PROMISE OF THE HAWTHORN

Spring sleeps and stirs and trembles with desire
Pure as a babe's that nestles toward the breast.
The world, as yet an all unstricken lyre,
With all its chords alive and all at rest,
Feels not the sun's hand yet, but feels his breath
And yearns for love made perfect. Man and bird,

Thrilled through with hope of life that casts out death,
Wait with a rapturous patience till his word
Speak heaven, and flower by flower and tree by tree
Give back the silent strenuous utterance. Earth,
Alive awhile and joyful as the sea,
Laughs not aloud in joy too deep for mirth,
Presageful of perfection of delight,
Till all the unborn green buds be born in white.

HAWTHORN TIDE

I

Dawn is alive in the world, and the darkness of heaven and of earth
Subsides in the light of a smile more sweet than the loud noon's mirth,
Spring lives as a babe lives, glad and divine as the sun, and unsure
If aught so divine and so glad may be worshipped and loved and endure.
A soft green glory suffuses the love-lit earth with delight,
And the face of the noon is fair as the face of the star-clothed night.
Earth knows not and doubts not at heart of the glories again to be:
Sleep doubts not and dreams not how sweet shall the waking beyond her be.
A whole white world of revival awaits May's whisper awhile,
Abides and exults in the bud as a soft hushed laugh in a smile.
As a maid's mouth laughing with love and subdued for the love's sake, May
Shines and withholds for a little the word she revives to say.

When the clouds and the winds and the sunbeams are warring and strengthening with joy that they live,
Spring, from reluctance enkindled to rapture, from slumber to strife,
Stirs, and repents, and is winter, and weeps, and awakes as the frosts forgive,
And the dark chill death of the woodland is troubled, and dies into life.
And the honey of heaven, of the hives whence night feeds full on the springtide's breath,
Fills fuller the lips of the lustrous air with delight in the dawn:
Each blossom enkindling with love that is life and subsides with a smile into death
Arises and lightens and sets as a star from her sphere withdrawn.
Not sleep, in the rapture of radiant dreams, when sundawn smiles on the night,
Shows earth so sweet with a splendour and fragrance of life that is love:
Each blade of the glad live grass, each bud that receives or rejects the light,
Salutes and responds to the marvel of Maytime around and above.

Joy gives thanks for the sight and the savour of heaven, and is humbled
With awe that exults in thanksgiving: the towers of the flowers of the trees
Shine sweeter than snows that the hand of the season has melted and crumbled,
And fair as the foam that is lesser of life than the loveliest of these.
But the sense of a life more lustrous with joy and enkindled of glory
Than man's was ever or may be, and briefer than joys most brief,
Bids man's heart bend and adore, be the man's head golden or hoary,

As it leapt but a breath's time since and saluted the flower and the leaf.
The rapture that springs into love at the sight of the world's exultation
Takes not a sense of rebuke from the sense of triumphant awe:
But the spirit that quickens the body fulfils it with mute adoration,
And the knees would fain bow down as the eyes that rejoiced and saw.

II

Fair and sublime as the face of the dawn is the splendour of May,
But the sky's and the sea's joy fades not as earth's pride passes away.
Yet hardly the sun's first lightning or laughter of love on the sea
So humbles the heart into worship that knows not or doubts if it be
As the first full glory beholden again of the life new-born
That hails and applauds with inaudible music the season of morn.
A day's length since, and it was not: a night's length more, and the sun
Salutes and enkindles a world of delight as a strange world won.
A new life answers and thrills to the kiss of the young strong year,
And the glory we see is as music we hear not, and dream that we hear.
From blossom to blossom the live tune kindles, from tree to tree,
And we know not indeed if we hear not the song of the life we see.

For the first blithe day that beholds it and worships and cherishes cannot but sing
With a louder and lustier delight in the sun and the sunlit earth
Than the joy of the days that beheld but the soft green dawn of the slow faint spring
Glad and afraid to be glad, and subdued in a shamefast mirth.
When the first bright knoll of the woodland world laughs out into fragrant light,
The year's heart changes and quickens with sense of delight in desire,
And the kindling desire is one with thanksgiving for utter fruition of sight,
For sight and for sense of a world that the sun finds meet for his lyre.
Music made of the morning that smites from the chords of the mute world song
Trembles and quickens and lightens, unfelt, unbeholden, unheard,
From blossom on blossom that climbs and exults in the strength of the sun grown strong,
And answers the word of the wind of the spring with the sun's own word.

Hard on the skirt of the deep soft copses that spring refashions,
Triumphs and towers to the height of the crown of a wildwood tree
One royal hawthorn, sublime and serene as the joy that impassions
Awe that exults in thanksgiving for sight of the grace we see,
The grace that is given of a god that abides for a season, mysterious
And merciful, fervent and fugitive, seen and unknown and adored:
His presence is felt in the light and the fragrance, elate and imperious,
His laugh and his breath in the blossom are love's, the beloved soul's lord.
For surely the soul if it loves is beloved of the god as a lover
Whose love is not all unaccepted, a worship not utterly vain:
So full, so deep is the joy that revives for the soul to recover
Yearly, beholden of hope and of memory in sunshine and rain.

III

Wonder and love stand silent, stricken at heart and stilled.
But yet is the cup of delight and of worship unpledged and unfilled.
A handsbreadth hence leaps up, laughs out as an angel crowned,
A strong full fountain of flowers overflowing above and around.
The boughs and the blossoms in triumph salute with adoring mirth
The womb that bare them, the glad green mother, the sunbright earth.
Downward sweeping, as song subsides into silence, none
May hear what sound is the word's they speak to the brooding sun.
None that hearken may hear: man may but pass and adore,
And humble his heart in thanksgiving for joy that is now no more.
And sudden, afront and ahead of him, joy is alive and aflame
On the shrine whose incense is given of the godhead, again the same.

Pale and pure as a maiden secluded in secret and cherished with fear,
One sweet glad hawthorn smiles as it shrinks under shelter, screened
By two strong brethren whose bounteous blossom outsoars it, year after year,
While earth still cleaves to the live spring's breast as a babe unweaned.
Never was amaranth fairer in fields where heroes of old found rest,
Never was asphodel sweeter: but here they endure not long,
Though ever the sight that salutes them again and adores them awhile is blest,
And the heart is a hymn, and the sense is a soul, and the soul is a song.
Alone on a dyke's trenched edge, and afar from the blossoming wildwood's verge,
Laughs and lightens a sister, triumphal in love-lit pride;
Clothed round with the sun, and inviolate: her blossoms exult as the springtide surge,
When the wind and the dawn enkindle the snows of the shoreward tide.

Hardly the worship of old that rejoiced as it knelt in the vision
Shown of the God new-born whose breath is the spirit of spring
Hailed ever with love more strong and defiant of death's derision
A joy more perfect than here we mourn for as May takes wing.
Time gives it and takes it again and restores it: the glory, the wonder,
The triumph of lustrous blossom that makes of the steep sweet bank
One visible marvel of music inaudible, over and under,
Attuned as in heaven, pass hence and return for the sun to thank.
The stars and the sun give thanks for the glory bestowed and beholden,
For the gladness they give and rejoice in, the night and the dawn and the day:
But nought they behold when the world is aflower and the season is golden
Makes answer as meet and as sweet as the flower that itself is May.

THE PASSING OF THE HAWTHORN

The coming of the hawthorn brings on earth
Heaven: all the spring speaks out in one sweet word,

And heaven grows gladder, knowing that earth has heard.
Ere half the flowers are jubilant in birth,
The splendour of the laughter of their mirth
Dazzles delight with wonder: man and bird
Rejoice and worship, stilled at heart and stirred
With rapture girt about with awe for girth.

The passing of the hawthorn takes away
Heaven: all the spring falls dumb, and all the soul
Sinks down in man for sorrow. Night and day
Forego the joy that made them one and whole.
The change that falls on every starry spray
Bids, flower by flower, the knell of springtime toll.

TO A BABY KINSWOMAN

Love, whose light thrills heaven and earth,
Smiles and weeps upon thy birth,
Child, whose mother's love-lit eyes
Watch thee but from Paradise.
Sweetest sight that earth can give,
Sweetest light of eyes that live,
Ours must needs, for hope withdrawn,
Hail with tears thy soft spring dawn.
Light of hope whose star hath set,
Light of love whose sun lives yet,
Holier, happier, heavenlier love
Breathes about thee, burns above,
Surely, sweet, than ours can be,
Shed from eyes we may not see,
Though thine own may see them shine
Night and day, perchance, on thine.
Sun and moon that lighten earth
Seem not fit to bless thy birth:
Scarce the very stars we know
Here seem bright enough to show
Whence in unimagined skies
Glows the vigil of such eyes.
Theirs whose heart is as a sea
Swoln with sorrowing love of thee
Fain would share with thine the sight
Seen alone of babes aright,
Watched of eyes more sweet than flowers
Sleeping or awake: but ours
Can but deem or dream or guess
Thee not wholly motherless.

Might they see or might they know
What nor faith nor hope may show,
We whose hearts yearn toward thee now
Then were blest and wise as thou.
Had we half thy knowledge,—had
Love such wisdom,—grief were glad,
Surely, lit by grace of thee;
Life were sweet as death may be.
Now the law that lies on men
Bids us mourn our dead: but then
Heaven and life and earth and death,
Quickened as by God's own breath,
All were turned from sorrow and strife:
Earth and death were heaven and life.
All too far are then and now
Sundered: none may be as thou.
Yet this grace is ours—a sign
Of that goodlier grace of thine,
Sweet, and thine alone—to see
Heaven, and heaven's own love, in thee.
Bless them, then, whose eyes caress
Thee, as only thou canst bless.
Comfort, faith, assurance, love,
Shine around us, brood above,
Fear grows hope, and hope grows wise,
Thrilled and lit by children's eyes.
Yet in ours the tears unshed,
Child, for hope that death leaves dead,
Needs must burn and tremble; thou
Knowest not, seest not, why nor how,
More than we know whence or why
Comes on babes that laugh and lie
Half asleep, in sweet-lipped scorn,
Light of smiles outlightening morn,
Whence enkindled as is earth
By the dawn's less radiant birth
All the body soft and sweet
Smiles on us from face to feet
When the rose-red hands would fain
Reach the rose-red feet in vain.
Eyes and hands that worship thee
Watch and tend, adore and see
All these heavenly sights, and give
Thanks to see and love and live.
Yet, of all that hold thee dear,
Sweet, the dearest smiles not here.
Thine alone is now the grace,
Haply, still to see her face;

Thine, thine only now the sight
Whence we dream thine own takes light.
Yet, though faith and hope live blind,
Yet they live in heart and mind
Strong and keen as truth may be:
Yet, though blind as grief were we
Inly for a weeping-while,
Sorrow's self before thy smile
Smiles and softens, knowing that yet,
Far from us though heaven be set,
Love, bowed down for thee to bless,
Dares not call thee motherless.

May 1894.

THE ALTAR OF RIGHTEOUSNESS

I

Light and night, whose clouds and glories change and mingle and divide,
Veil the truth whereof they witness, show the truth of things they hide.
Through the darkness and the splendour of the centuries, loud or dumb,
Shines and wanes and shines the spirit, lit with love of life to come.
Man, the soul made flesh, that knows not death from life, and fain would know,
Sees the face of time change colour as its tides recoil and flow.
All his hope and fear and faith and doubt, if aught at all they be,
Live the life of clouds and sunbeams, born of heaven or earth or sea.
All are buoyed and blown and brightened by their hour's evasive breath:
All subside and quail and darken when their hour is done to death.
Yet, ere faith, a wandering water, froze and curdled into creeds,
Earth, elate as heaven, adored the light that quickens dreams to deeds.

Invisible: eye hath not seen it, and ear hath not heard as the spirit hath heard
From the shrine that is lit not of sunlight or starlight the sound of a limitless word.
And visible: none that hath eyes to behold what the spirit must perish or see
Can choose but behold it and worship: a shrine that if light were as darkness would be.
Of cloud and of change is the form of the fashion that man may behold of it wrought:
Of iron and truth is the mystic mid altar, where worship is none but of thought.
No prayer may go up to it, climbing as incense of gladness or sorrow may climb:
No rapture of music may ruffle the silence that guards it, and hears not of time.
As the winds of the wild blind ages alternate in passion of light and of cloud,
So changes the shape of the veil that enshrouds it with darkness and light for a shroud.
And the winds and the clouds and the suns fall silent, and fade out of hearing or sight,
And the shrine stands fast and is changed not, whose likeness was changed as a cloud in the night.

All the storms of time, and wrath of many winds, may carve no trace

On the viewless altar, though the veil bear many a name and face:
Many a live God's likeness woven, many a scripture dark with awe,
Bids the veil seem verier iron than the word of life's own law.
Till the might of change hath rent it with a rushing wind in twain,
Stone or steel it seems, whereon the wrath of chance is wreaked in vain:
Stone or steel, and all behind it or beyond its lifted sign
Cloud and vapour, no subsistence of a change-unstricken shrine.
God by god flits past in thunder, till his glories turn to shades:
God to god bears wondering witness how his gospel flames and fades.
More was each of these, while yet they were, than man their servant seemed:
Dead are all of these, and man survives who made them while he dreamed.

Yet haply or surely, if vision were surer than theirs who rejoiced that they saw,
Man might not but see, through the darkness of godhead, the light that is surety and law.
On the stone that the close-drawn cloud which veils it awhile makes cloudlike stands
The word of the truth everlasting, unspoken of tongues and unwritten of hands.
By the sunbeams and storms of the centuries engraven, and approved of the soul as it reads,
It endures as a token dividing the light from the darkness of dreams and of deeds.
The faces of gods on the face of it carven, or gleaming behind and above,
Star-glorified Uranus, thunderous Jehovah, for terror or worship or love,
Change, wither, and brighten as flowers that the wind of eternity sheds upon time,
All radiant and transient and awful and mortal, and leave it unmarred and sublime.
As the tides that return and recede are the fears and the hopes of the centuries that roll,
Requenched and rekindled: but strong as the sun is the sense of it shrined in the soul.

II

In the days when time was not, in the time when days were none,
Ere sorrow had life to lot, ere earth gave thanks for the sun,
Ere man in his darkness waking adored what the soul in him could,
And the manifold God of his making was manifest evil and good,
One law from the dim beginning abode and abides in the end,
In sight of him sorrowing and sinning with none but his faith for friend.
Dark were the shadows around him, and darker the glories above,
Ere light from beyond them found him, and bade him for love's sake love.
About him was darkness, and under and over him darkness: the night
That conceived him and bore him had thunder for utterance and lightning for light.
The dust of death was the dust of the ways that the tribes of him trod:
And he knew not if just or unjust were the might of the mystery of God.
Strange horror and hope, strange faith and unfaith, were his boon and his bane:
And the God of his trust was the wraith of the soul or the ghost of it slain.
A curse was on death as on birth, and a Presence that shone as a sword
Shed menace from heaven upon earth that beheld him, and hailed him her Lord.
Sublime and triumphant as fire or as lightning, he kindled the skies,
And withered with dread the desire that would look on the light of his eyes.
Earth shuddered with worship, and knew not if hell were not hot in her breath;
If birth were not sin, and the dew of the morning the sweat of her death.

The watchwords of evil and good were unspoken of men and unheard:
They were shadows that willed as he would, that were made and unmade by his word.
His word was darkness and light, and a wisdom that makes men mad
Sent blindness upon them for sight, that they saw but and heard as he bade.
Cast forth and corrupt from the birth by the crime of creation, they stood
Convicted of evil on earth by the grace of a God found good.
The grace that enkindled and quickened the darkness of hell with flame
Bade man, though the soul in him sickened, obey, and give praise to his name.
The still small voice of the spirit whose life is as plague's hot breath
Bade man shed blood, and inherit the life of the kingdom of death.

"Bring now for blood-offering thy son to mine altar, and bind him and slay,
That the sin of my bidding be done": and the soul in the slave said, "Yea."
Yea, not nay, was the word: and the sacrifice offered withal
Was neither of beast nor of bird, but the soul of a man, God's thrall.
And the word of his servant spoken was fire, and the light of a sword,
When the bondage of Israel was broken, and Sinai shrank from the Lord.
With splendour of slaughter and thunder of song as the sound of the sea
Were the foes of him stricken in sunder and silenced as storms that flee.
Terror and trust and the pride of the chosen, approved of his choice,
Saw God in the whirlwind ride, and rejoiced as the winds rejoice.
Subdued and exalted and kindled and quenched by the sense of his might,
Faith flamed and exulted and dwindled, and saw not, and clung to the sight.
The wastes of the wilderness brightened and trembled with rapture and dread
When the word of him thundered and lightened and spake through the quick and the dead.
The chant of the prophetess, louder and loftier than tempest and wave,
Rang triumph more ruthless and prouder than death, and profound as the grave.
And sweet as the moon's word spoken in smiles that the blown clouds mar
The psalmist's witness in token arose as the speech of a star.
Starlight supreme, and the tender desire of the moon, were as one
To rebuke with compassion the splendour and strength of the god-like sun.
God softened and changed: and the word of his chosen, a fire at the first,
Bade man, as a beast or a bird, now slake at the springs his thirst.
The souls that were sealed unto death as the bones of the dead lie sealed
Rose thrilled and redeemed by the breath of the dawn on theflame-lit field.
The glories of darkness, cloven with music of thunder, shrank
As the web of the word was unwoven that spake, and the soul's tide sank.
And the starshine of midnight that covered Arabia with light as a robe
Waxed fiery with utterance that hovered and flamed through the whirlwind on Job.
And prophet to prophet and vision to vision made answer sublime,
Till the valley of doom and decision was merged in the tides of time.

III

Then, soft as the dews of night,
As the star of the sundawn bright,
As the heart of the sea's hymn deep,

And sweet as the balm of sleep,
Arose on the world a light
Too pure for the skies to keep.

With music sweeter and stranger than heaven had heard
When the dark east thrilled with light from a saviour's word
And a God grew man to endure as a man and abide
The doom of the will of the Lord of the loud world's tide,
Whom thunders utter, and tempest and darkness hide,
With larger light than flamed from the peak whereon
Prometheus, bound as the sun to the world's wheel, shone,
A presence passed and abode but on earth a span,
And love's own light as a river before him ran,
And the name of God for awhile upon earth was man.

O star that wast not and wast for the world a sun,
O light that was quenched of priests, and its work undone,
O Word that wast not as man's or as God's, if God
Be Lord but of hosts whose tread was as death's that trod
On souls that felt but his wrath as an unseen rod,
What word, what praise, what passion of hopeless prayer,
May now rise up to thee, loud as in years that were,
From years that gaze on the works of thy servants wrought
While strength was in them to satiate the lust of thought
That craved in thy name for blood as the quest it sought?

From the dark high places of Rome
Far over the westward foam
God's heaven and the sun saw swell
The fires of the high priest's hell,
And shrank as they curled and clomb
And revelled and ravaged and fell.

IV

Yet was not the work of thy word all withered with wasting flame
By the sons of the priests that had slain thee, whose evil was wrought in thy name.
From the blood-sodden soil that was blasted with fires of the Church and her creed
Sprang rarely but surely, by grace of thy spirit, a flower for a weed.
Thy spirit, unfelt of thy priests who blasphemed thee, enthralled and enticed
To deathward a child that was even as the child we behold in Christ.
The Moors, they told her, beyond bright Spain and the strait brief sea,
Dwelt blind in the light that for them was as darkness, and knew not thee.
But the blood of the martyrs whose mission was witness for God, they said,
Might raise to redemption the souls that were here, in the sun's sight, dead.
And the child rose up in the night, when the stars were as friends that smiled,
And sought her brother, and wakened the younger and tenderer child.

From the heaven of a child's glad sleep to the heaven of the sight of her eyes
He woke, and brightened and hearkened, and kindled as stars that rise.
And forth they fared together to die for the stranger's sake,
For the souls of the slayers that should slay them, and turn from their sins, and wake.
And the light of the love that lit them awhile on a brief blind quest
Shines yet on the tear-lit smile that salutes them, belated and blest.

And the girl, full-grown to the stature of godhead in womanhood, spake
The word that sweetens and lightens her creed for her great love's sake.
From the godlike heart of Theresa the prayer above all prayers heard,
The cry as of God made woman, a sweet blind wonderful word,
Sprang sudden as flame, and kindled the darkness of faith with love,
And the hollow of hell from beneath shone, quickened of heaven from above.
Yea, hell at her word grew heaven, as she prayed that if God thought well
She there might stand in the gateway, that none might pass into hell.
Not Hermes, guardian and guide, God, herald, and comforter, shed
Such lustre of hope from the life of his light on the night of the dead.
Not Pallas, wiser and mightier in mercy than Rome's God shone,
Wore ever such raiment of love as the soul of a saint put on.
So blooms as a flower of the darkness a star of the midnight born,
Of the midnight's womb and the blackness of darkness, and flames like morn.
Nor yet may the dawn extinguish or hide it, when churches and creeds
Are withered and blasted with sunlight as poisonous and blossomless weeds.
So springs and strives through the soil that the legions of darkness have trod,
From the root that is man, from the soul in the body, the flower that is God.

V

Ages and creeds that drift
Through change and cloud uplift
The soul that soars and seeks her sovereign shrine,
Her faith's veiled altar, there
To find, when praise and prayer
Fall baffled, if the darkness be divine.
Lights change and shift through star and sun:
Night, clothed with might of immemorial years, is one.

Day, born and slain of night,
Hath hardly life in sight
As she that bears and slays him and survives,
And gives us back for one
Cloud-thwarted fiery sun
The myriad mysteries of the lambent lives
Whose starry soundless music saith
That light and life wax perfect even through night and death.

In vain had darkness heard

Light speak the lustrous word
That cast out faith in all save truth and love:
In vain death's quickening rod
Bade man rise up as God,
Touched as with life unknown in heaven above:
Fear turned his light of love to fire
That wasted earth, yet might not slay the soul's desire.

Though death seem life, and night
Bid fear call darkness light,
Time, faith, and hope keep trust, through sorrow and shame,
Till Christ, by Paul cast out,
Return, and all the rout
Of raging slaves whose prayer defiles his name
Rush headlong to the deep, and die,
And leave no sign to say that faith once heard them lie.

VI

Since man, with a child's pride proud, and abashed as a child and afraid,
Made God in his likeness, and bowed him to worship the Maker he made,
No faith more dire hath enticed man's trust than the saint's whose creed
Made Caiaphas one with Christ, that worms on the cross might feed.
Priests gazed upon God in the eyes of a babe new-born, and therein
Beheld not heaven, and the wise glad secret of love, but sin.
Accursed of heaven, and baptized with the baptism of hatred and hell,
They spat on the name they despised and adored as a sign and a spell.
"Lord Christ, thou art God, and a liar: they were children of wrath, not of grace,
Unbaptized, unredeemed from the fire they were born for, who smiled in thy face."
Of such is the kingdom—he said it—of heaven: and the heavenly word
Shall live when religion is dead, and when falsehood is dumb shall be heard.
And the message of James and of John was as Christ's and as love's own call:
But wrath passed sentence thereon when Annas replied in Paul.
The dark old God who had slain him grew one with the Christ he slew,
And poison was rank in the grain that with growth of his gospel grew.
And the blackness of darkness brightened: and red in the heart of the flame
Shone down, as a blessing that lightened, the curse of a new God's name.
Through centuries of burning and trembling belief as a signal it shone,
Till man, soul-sick of dissembling, bade fear and her frauds begone.
God Cerberus yelps from his throats triune: but his day, which was night,
Is quenched, with its stars and the notes of its night-birds, in silence and light.
The flames of its fires and the psalms of their psalmists are darkened and dumb:
Strong winter has withered the palms of his angels, and stricken them numb.
God, father of lies, God, son of perdition, God, spirit of ill,
Thy will that for ages was done is undone as a dead God's will.
Not Mahomet's sword could slay thee, nor Borgia's or Calvin's praise:
But the scales of the spirit that weigh thee are weighted with truth, and it slays.

The song of the day of thy fury, when nature and death shall quail,
Rings now as the thunders of Jewry, the ghost of a dead world's tale.
That day and its doom foreseen and foreshadowed on earth, when thou,
Lord God, wast lord of the keen dark season, are sport for us now.
Thy claws were clipped and thy fangs plucked out by the hands that slew
Men, lovers of man, whose pangs bore witness if truth were true.
Man crucified rose again from the sepulchre builded to be
No grave for the souls of the men who denied thee, but, Lord, for thee.

When Bruno's spirit aspired from the flames that thy servants fed,
The spirit of faith was fired to consume thee and leave thee dead.
When the light of the sunlike eyes whence laughter lightened and flamed
Bade France and the world be wise, faith saw thee naked and shamed.
When wisdom deeper and sweeter than Rabelais veiled and revealed
Found utterance diviner and meeter for truth whence anguish is healed,
Whence fear and hate and belief in thee, fed by thy grace from above,
Fall stricken, and utmost grief takes light from the lustre of love,
When Shakespeare shone into birth, and the world he beheld grew bright,
Thy kingdom was ended on earth, and the darkness it shed was light.
In him all truth and the glory thereof and the power and the pride,
The song of the soul and her story, bore witness that fear had lied.
All hope, all wonder, all trust, all doubt that knows not of fear,
The love of the body, the lust of the spirit to see and to hear,
All womanhood, fairer than love could conceive or desire or adore,
All manhood, radiant above all heights that it held of yore,
Lived by the life of his breath, with the speech of his soul's will spake,
And the light lit darkness to death whence never the dead shall wake.
For the light that lived in the sound of the song of his speech was one
With the light of the wisdom that found earth's tune in the song of the sun;
His word with the word of the lord most high of us all on earth,
Whose soul was a lyre and a sword, whose death was a deathless birth.
Him too we praise as we praise our own who as he stand strong;
Him, Æschylus, ancient of days, whose word is the perfect song.
When Caucasus showed to the sun and the sea what a God could endure,
When wisdom and light were one, and the hands of the matricide pure,
A song too subtle for psalmist or prophet of Jewry to know,
Elate and profound as the calmest or stormiest of waters that flow,
A word whose echoes were wonder and music of fears overcome,
Bade Sinai bow, and the thunder of godhead on Horeb be dumb.
The childless children of night, strong daughters of doom and dread,
The thoughts and the fears that smite the soul, and its life lies dead,
Stood still and were quelled by the sound of his word and the light of his thought,
And the God that in man lay bound was unbound from the bonds he had wrought.
Dark fear of a lord more dark than the dreams of his worshippers knew
Fell dead, and the corpse lay stark in the sunlight of truth shown true.

VII

Time, and truth his child, though terror set earth and heaven at odds,
See the light of manhood rise on the twilight of the Gods.
Light is here for souls to see, though the stars of faith be dead:
All the sea that yearned and trembled receives the sun instead.
All the shadows on the spirit when fears and dreams were strong,
All perdition, all redemption, blind rain-stars watched so long,
Love whose root was fear, thanksgiving that cowered beneath the rod,
Feel the light that heals and withers: night weeps upon her God.
All the names wherein the incarnate Lord lived his day and died
Fade from suns to stars, from stars into darkness undescried.

Christ the man lives yet, remembered of man as dreams that leave
Light on eyes that wake and know not if memory bid them grieve.
Fire sublime as lightning shines, and exults in thunder yet,
Where the battle wields the name and the sword of Mahomet.
Far above all wars and gospels, all ebb and flow of time,
Lives the soul that speaks in silence, and makes mute earth sublime.
Still for her, though years and ages be blinded and bedinned,
Mazed with lightnings, crazed with thunders, life rides and guides the wind.
Death may live or death may die, and the truth be light or night:
Not for gain of heaven may man put away the rule of right.

A NEW YEAR'S EVE

CHRISTINA ROSSETTI DIED DECEMBER 29, 1894

The stars are strong in the deeps of the lustrous night,
Cold and splendid as death if his dawn be bright;
Cold as the cast-off garb that is cold as clay,
Splendid and strong as a spirit intense as light.

A soul more sweet than the morning of new-born May
Has passed with the year that has passed from the world away.
A song more sweet than the morning's first-born song
Again will hymn not among us a new year's day.

Not here, not here shall the carol of joy grown strong
Ring rapture now, and uplift us, a spell-struck throng,
From dream to vision of life that the soul may see
By death's grace only, if death do its trust no wrong.

Scarce yet the days and the starry nights are three
Since here among us a spirit abode as we,
Girt round with life that is fettered in bonds of time,
And clasped with darkness about as is earth with sea.

And now, more high than the vision of souls may climb,
The soul whose song was as music of stars that chime,
Clothed round with life as of dawn and the mounting sun,
Sings, and we know not here of the song sublime.

No word is ours of it now that the songs are done
Whence here we drank of delight as in freedom won,
In deep deliverance given from the bonds we bore.
There is none to sing as she sang upon earth, not one.

We heard awhile: and for us who shall hear no more
The sound as of waves of light on a starry shore
Awhile bade brighten and yearn as a father's face
The face of death, divine as in days of yore.

The grey gloom quickened and quivered: the sunless place
Thrilled, and the silence deeper than time or space
Seemed now not all everlasting. Hope grew strong,
And love took comfort, given of the sweet song's grace.

Love that finds not on earth, where it finds but wrong,
Love that bears not the bondage of years in throng
Shone to show for her, higher than the years that mar,
The life she looked and longed for as love must long.

Who knows? We know not. Afar, if the dead be far,
Alive, if the dead be alive as the soul's works are,
The soul whose breath was among us a heavenward song
Sings, loves, and shines as it shines for us here a star.

IN A ROSARY

Through the low grey archway children's feet that pass
Quicken, glad to find the sweetest haunt of all.
Brightest wildflowers gleaming deep in lustiest grass,
Glorious weeds that glisten through the green sea's glass,
Match not now this marvel, born to fade and fall.

Roses like a rainbow wrought of roses rise
Right and left and forward, shining toward the sun.
Nay, the rainbow lit of sunshine droops and dies
Ere we dream it hallows earth and seas and skies;
Ere delight may dream it lives, its life is done.

Round the border hemmed with high deep hedges round

Go the children, peering over or between
Where the dense bright oval wall of box inwound,
Reared about the roses fast within it bound,
Gives them grace to glance at glories else unseen.

Flower outlightening flower and tree outflowering tree
Feed and fill the sense and spirit full with joy.
Nought awhile they know of outer earth and sea:
Here enough of joy it is to breathe and be:
Here the sense of life is one for girl and boy.

Heaven above them, bright as children's eyes or dreams,
Earth about them, sweet as glad soft sleep can show
Earth and sky and sea, a world that scarcely seems
Even in children's eyes less fair than life that gleams
Through the sleep that none but sinless eyes may know.

Near beneath, and near above, the terraced ways
Wind or stretch and bask or blink against the sun.
Hidden here from sight on soft or stormy days
Lies and laughs with love toward heaven, at silent gaze,
All the radiant rosary—all its flowers made one.

All the multitude of roses towering round
Dawn and noon and night behold as one full flower,
Fain of heaven and loved of heaven, curbed and crowned,
Raised and reared to make this plot of earthly ground
Heavenly, could but heaven endure on earth an hour.

Swept away, made nothing now for ever, dead,
Still the rosary lives and shines on memory, free
Now from fear of death or change as childhood, fled
Years on years before its last live leaves were shed:
None may mar it now, as none may stain the sea.

THE HIGH OAKS

BARKING HALL, JULY 19TH, 1896

Fourscore years and seven
Light and dew from heaven
Have fallen with dawn on these glad woods each day
Since here was born, even here,
A birth more bright and dear
Than ever a younger year
Hath seen or shall till all these pass away,

Even all the imperious pride of these,
The woodland ways majestic now with towers of trees.

Love itself hath nought
Touched of tenderest thought
With holiest hallowing of memorial grace
For memory, blind with bliss,
To love, to clasp, to kiss,
So sweetly strange as this,
The sense that here the sun first hailed her face,
A babe at Her glad mother's breast,
And here again beholds it more beloved and blest.

Love's own heart, a living
Spring of strong thanksgiving,
Can bid no strength of welling song find way
When all the soul would seek
One word for joy to speak,
And even its strength makes weak
The too strong yearning of the soul to say
What may not be conceived or said
While darkness makes division of the quick and dead.

Haply, where the sun
Wanes, and death is none,
The word known here of silence only, held
Too dear for speech to wrong,
May leap in living song
Forth, and the speech be strong
As here the silence whence it yearned and welled
From hearts whose utterance love sealed fast
Till death perchance might give it grace to live at last.

Here we have our earth
Yet, with all the mirth
Of all the summers since the world began,
All strengths of rest and strife
And love-lit love of life
Where death has birth to wife,
And where the sun speaks, and is heard of man:
Yea, half the sun's bright speech is heard,
And like the sea the soul of man gives back his word.

Earth's enkindled heart
Bears benignant part
In the ardent heaven's auroral pride of prime:
If ever home on earth
Were found of heaven's grace worth

So God-beloved a birth
As here makes bright the fostering face of time,
Here, heaven bears witness, might such grace
Fall fragrant as the dewfall on that brightening face.

Here, for mine and me,
All that eyes may see
Hath more than all the wide world else of good,
All nature else of fair:
Here as none otherwhere
Heaven is the circling air,
Heaven is the homestead, heaven the wold, the wood:
The fragrance with the shadow spread
From broadening wings of cedars breathes of dawn's bright bed.

Once a dawn rose here
More divine and dear,
Rose on a birth-bed brighter far than dawn's,
Whence all the summer grew
Sweet as when earth was new
And pure as Eden's dew:
And yet its light lives on these lustrous lawns,
Clings round these wildwood ways, and cleaves
To the aisles of shadow and sun that wind unweaves and weaves.

Thoughts that smile and weep,
Dreams that hallow sleep,
Brood in the branching shadows of the trees,
Tall trees at agelong rest
Wherein the centuries nest,
Whence, blest as these are blest,
We part, and part not from delight in these;
Whose comfort, sleeping as awake,
We bear about within us as when first it spake.

Comfort as of song
Grown with time more strong,
Made perfect and prophetic as the sea,
Whose message, when it lies
Far off our hungering eyes,
Within us prophesies
Of life not ours, yet ours as theirs may be
Whose souls far off us shine and sing
As ere they sprang back sunward, swift as fire might spring.

All this oldworld pleasance
Hails a hallowing presence,
And thrills with sense of more than summer near,

And lifts toward heaven more high
The song-surpassing cry
Of rapture that July
Lives, for her love who makes it loveliest here;
For joy that she who here first drew
The breath of life she gave me breathes it here anew.

Never birthday born
Highest in height of morn
Whereout the star looks forth that leads the sun
Shone higher in love's account,
Still seeing the mid noon mount
From the eager dayspring's fount
Each year more lustrous, each like all in one;
Whose light around us and above
We could not see so lovely save by grace of love.

BARKING HALL: A YEAR AFTER

Still the sovereign trees
Make the sundawn's breeze
More bright, more sweet, more heavenly than it rose,
As wind and sun fulfil
Their living rapture: still
Noon, dawn, and evening thrill
With radiant change the immeasurable repose
Wherewith the woodland wilds lie blest
And feel how storms and centuries rock them still to rest.

Still the love-lit place
Given of God such grace
That here was born on earth a birth divine
Gives thanks with all its flowers
Through all their lustrous hours,
From all its birds and bowers
Gives thanks that here they felt her sunset shine
Where once her sunrise laughed, and bade
The life of all the living things it lit be glad.

Soft as light and strong
Rises yet their song
And thrills with pride the cedar-crested lawn
And every brooding dove.
But she, beloved above
All utterance known of love,
Abides no more the change of night and dawn,

Beholds no more with earth-born eye
These woods that watched her waking here where all things die.

Not the light that shone
When she looked thereon
Shines on them or shall shine for ever here.
We know not, save when sleep
Slays death, who fain would keep
His mystery dense and deep,
Where shines the smile we held and hold so dear.
Dreams only, thrilled and filled with love,
Bring back its light ere dawn leave nought alive above.

Nought alive awake
Sees the strong dawn break
On all the dreams that dying night bade live.
Yet scarce the intolerant sense
Of day's harsh evidence
How came their word and whence
Strikes dumb the song of thanks it bids them give,
The joy that answers as it heard
And lightens as it saw the light that spake the word.

Night and sleep and dawn
Pass with dreams withdrawn:
But higher above them far than noon may climb
Love lives and turns to light
The deadly noon of night.
His fiery spirit of sight
Endures no curb of change or darkling time.
Even earth and transient things of earth
Even here to him bear witness not of death but birth.

MUSIC: AN ODE

I

Was it light that spake from the darkness, or music that shone from the word,
When the night was enkindled with sound of the sun or the first-born bird?
Souls enthralled and entrammelled in bondage of seasons that fall and rise,
Bound fast round with the fetters of flesh, and blinded with light that dies,
Lived not surely till music spake, and the spirit of life was heard.

II

Music, sister of sunrise, and herald of life to be,
Smiled as dawn on the spirit of man, and the thrall was free.
Slave of nature and serf of time, the bondman of life and death,
Dumb with passionless patience that breathed but forlorn and reluctant breath,
Heard, beheld, and his soul made answer, and communed aloud with the sea.

III

Morning spake, and he heard: and the passionate silent noon
Kept for him not silence: and soft from the mounting moon
Fell the sound of her splendour, heard as dawn's in the breathless night,
Not of men but of birds whose note bade man's soul quicken and leap to light:
And the song of it spake, and the light and the darkness of earth were as chords in tune.

THE CENTENARY OF THE BATTLE OF THE NILE

AUGUST 1898

'Horatio Nelson—Honor est a Nilo'

A hundred years have lightened and have waned
Since ancient Nile by grace of Nelson gained
A glory higher in story now than time
Saw when his kings were gods that raged and reigned.

The day that left even England more sublime
And higher on heights that none but she may climb
Abides above all shock of change-born chance
Where hope and memory hear the stars keep chime.

The strong and sunbright lie whose name was France
Arose against the sun of truth, whose glance
Laughed large from the eyes of England, fierce as fire
Whence eyes wax blind that gaze on truth askance.

A name above all names of heroes, higher
Than song may sound or heart of man aspire,
Rings as the very voice that speaks the sea
To-day from all the sea's enkindling lyre.

The sound that bids the soul of silence be
Fire, and a rapturous music, speaks, and we
Hear what the sea's heart utters, wide and far:
"This was his day, and this day's light was he."

O sea, our sea that hadst him for thy star,
A hundred years that fall upon thee are
Even as a hundred flakes of rain or snow:
No storm of battle signs thee with a scar.

But never more may ship that sails thee show,
But never may the sun that loves thee know,
But never may thine England give thee more,
A man whose life and death shall praise thee so.

The Nile, the sea, the battle, and the shore,
Heard as we hear one word arise and soar,
Beheld one name above them tower and glow—
Nelson: a light that time bows down before.

TRAFALGAR DAY

Sea, that art ours as we are thine, whose name
Is one with England's even as light with flame,
Dost thou as we, thy chosen of all men, know
This day of days when death gave life to fame?

Dost thou not kindle above and thrill below
With rapturous record, with memorial glow,
Remembering this thy festal day of fight,
And all the joy it gave, and all the woe?

Never since day broke flowerlike forth of night
Broke such a dawn of battle. Death in sight
Made of the man whose life was like the sun
A man more godlike than the lord of light.

There is none like him, and there shall be none.
When England bears again as great a son,
He can but follow fame where Nelson led.
There is not and there cannot be but one.

As earth has but one England, crown and head
Of all her glories till the sun be dead,
Supreme in peace and war, supreme in song,
Supreme in freedom, since her rede was read,

Since first the soul that gave her speech grew strong
To help the right and heal the wild world's wrong,
So she hath but one royal Nelson, born
To reign on time above the years that throng.

The music of his name puts fear to scorn,
And thrills our twilight through with sense of morn:
As England was, how should not England be?
No tempest yet has left her banner torn.

No year has yet put out the day when he
Who lived and died to keep our kingship free
Wherever seas by warring winds are worn
Died, and was one with England and the sea.

October 21, 1895.

CROMWELL'S STATUE[1]

What needs our Cromwell stone or bronze to say
His was the light that lit on England's way
The sundawn of her time-compelling power,
The noontide of her most imperial day?

His hand won back the sea for England's dower;
His footfall bade the Moor change heart and cower;
His word on Milton's tongue spake law to France
When Piedmont felt the she-wolf Rome devour.

From Cromwell's eyes the light of England's glance
Flashed, and bowed down the kings by grace of chance,
The priest-anointed princes; one alone
By grace of England held their hosts in trance.

The enthroned Republic from her kinglier throne
Spake, and her speech was Cromwell's. Earth has known
No lordlier presence. How should Cromwell stand
With kinglets and with queenlings hewn in stone?

Incarnate England in his warrior hand
Smote, and as fire devours the blackening brand
Made ashes of their strengths who wrought her wrong,
And turned the strongholds of her foes to sand.

His praise is in the sea's and Milton's song;
What praise could reach him from the weakling throng
That rules by leave of tongues whose praise is shame—
Him, who made England out of weakness strong?

There needs no clarion's blast of broad-blown fame

To bid the world bear witness whence he came
Who bade fierce Europe fawn at England's heel
And purged the plague of lineal rule with flame.

There needs no witness graven on stone or steel
For one whose work bids fame bow down and kneel;
Our man of men, whose time-commanding name
Speaks England, and proclaims her Commonweal.

June 20, 1895.

[Footnote 1: Refused by the party of reaction and disunion in the House of Commons on the 17th of June, 1895.]

A WORD FOR THE NAVY

I

Queen born of the sea, that hast borne her
The mightiest of seamen on earth,
Bright England, whose glories adorn her
And bid her rejoice in thy birth
As others made mothers
Rejoice in births sublime,
She names thee, she claims thee,
The lordliest child of time.

II

All hers is the praise of thy story,
All thine is the love of her choice
The light of her waves is thy glory,
The sound of thy soul is her voice.
They fear it who hear it
And love not truth nor thee:
They sicken, heart-stricken,
Who see and would not see.

III

The lords of thy fate, and thy keepers
Whose charge is the strength of thy ships,
If now they be dreamers and sleepers,

Or sluggards with lies at their lips,
Thy haters and traitors,
False friends or foes descried,
Might scatter and shatter
Too soon thy princely pride.

IV

Dark Muscovy, reptile in rancour,
Base Germany, blatant in guile,
Lay wait for thee riding at anchor
On waters that whisper and smile.
They deem thee or dream thee
Less living now than dead,
Deep sunken and drunken
With sleep whence fear has fled.

V

And what though thy song as thine action
Wax faint, and thy place be not known,
While faction is grappling with faction,
Twin curs with thy corpse for a bone?
They care not, who spare not
The noise of pens or throats;
Who bluster and muster
Blind ranks and bellowing votes.

VI

Let populace jangle with peerage
And ministers shuffle their mobs;
Mad pilots who reck not of steerage
Though tempest ahead of them throbs.
That throbbing and sobbing
Of wind and gradual wave
They hear not and fear not
Who guide thee toward thy grave.

VII

No clamour of cries or of parties
Is worth but a whisper from thee,
While only the trust of thy heart is

At one with the soul of the sea.
In justice her trust is
Whose time her tidestreams keep;
They sink not, they shrink not,
Time casts them not on sleep.

Sleep thou: for thy past was so royal,
Love hardly would bid thee take heed
Were Russia not faithful and loyal
Nor Germany guiltless of greed.
No nation, in station
Of story less than thou,
Re-risen from prison,
Can stand against thee now.

Sleep on: is the time not a season
For strong men to slumber and sleep,
And wise men to palter with treason?
And that they sow tares, shall they reap?
The wages of ages
Wherein men smiled and slept,
Fame fails them, shame veils them,
Their record is not kept.

Nay, whence is it then that we know it,
What wages were theirs, and what fame?
Deep voices of prophet and poet
Bear record against them of shame.
Death, starker and darker
Than seals the graveyard grate,
Entombs them and dooms them
To darkness deep as fate.

But thou, though the world should misdoubt thee,
Be strong as the seas at thy side;
Bind on but thine armour about thee,

That girds thee with power and with pride.
Where Drake stood, where Blake stood,
Where fame sees Nelson stand,
Stand thou too, and now too
Take thou thy fate in hand.

XII

At the gate of the sea, in the gateway,
They stood as the guards of thy gate;
Take now but thy strengths to thee straightway,
Though late, we will deem it not late.
Thy story, thy glory,
The very soul of thee,
It rose not, it grows not,
It comes not save by sea.

NORTHUMBERLAND

Between our eastward and our westward sea
The narrowing strand
Clasps close the noblest shore fame holds in fee
Even here where English birth seals all men free—
Northumberland.

The sea-mists meet across it when the snow
Clothes moor and fell,
And bid their true-born hearts who love it glow
For joy that none less nobly born may know
What love knows well.

The splendour and the strength of storm and fight
Sustain the song
That filled our fathers' hearts with joy to smite,
To live, to love, to lay down life that right
Might tread down wrong.

They warred, they sang, they triumphed, and they passed,
And left us glad
Here to be born, their sons, whose hearts hold fast
The proud old love no change can overcast,
No chance leave sad.

None save our northmen ever, none but we,
Met, pledged, or fought

Such foes and friends as Scotland and the sea
With heart so high and equal, strong in glee
And stern in thought.

Thought, fed from time's memorial springs with pride,
Made strong as fire
Their hearts who hurled the foe down Flodden side,
And hers who rode the waves none else durst ride—
None save her sire.

O land beloved, where nought of legend's dream
Outshines the truth,
Where Joyous Gard, closed round with clouds that gleam
For them that know thee not, can scarce but seem
Too sweet for sooth,

Thy sons forget not, nor shall fame forget,
The deed there done
Before the walls whose fabled fame is yet
A light too sweet and strong to rise and set
With moon and sun.

Song bright as flash of swords or oars that shine
Through fight or foam
Stirs yet the blood thou hast given thy sons like wine
To hail in each bright ballad hailed as thine
One heart, one home.

Our Collingwood, though Nelson be not ours,
By him shall stand
Immortal, till those waifs of oldworld hours,
Forgotten, leave uncrowned with bays and flowers
Northumberland.

STRATFORD-ON-AVON

JUNE 27, 1901

Be glad in heaven above all souls insphered,
Most royal and most loyal born of men,
Shakespeare, of all on earth beloved or feared
Or worshipped, highest in sight of human ken.
The homestead hallowed by thy sovereign birth,
Whose name, being one with thine, stands higher than Rome,
Forgets not how of all on English earth
Their trust is holiest, there who have their home.

Stratford is thine and England's. None that hate
The commonweal whose empire sets men free
Find comfort there, where once by grace of fate
A soul was born as boundless as the sea.
If life, if love, if memory now be thine,
Rejoice that still thy Stratford bears thy sign.

BURNS: AN ODE

A fire of fierce and laughing light
That clove the shuddering heart of night
Leapt earthward, and the thunder's might
That pants and yearns
Made fitful music round its flight:
And earth saw Burns.

The joyous lightning found its voice
And bade the heart of wrath rejoice
And scorn uplift a song to voice
The imperial hate
That smote the God of base men's choice
At God's own gate.

Before the shrine of dawn, wherethrough
The lark rang rapture as she flew,
It flashed and fired the darkling dew:
And all that heard
With love or loathing hailed anew
A new day's word.

The servants of the lord of hell,
As though their lord had blessed them, fell
Foaming at mouth for fear, so well
They knew the lie
Wherewith they sought to scan and spell
The unsounded sky.

And Calvin, night's prophetic bird,
Out of his home in hell was heard
Shrieking; and all the fens were stirred
Whence plague is bred;
Can God endure the scoffer's word?
But God was dead.

The God they made them in despite
Of man and woman, love and light,

Strong sundawn and the starry night,
The lie supreme,
Shot through with song, stood forth to sight
A devil's dream.

And he that bent the lyric bow
And laid the lord of darkness low
And bade the fire of laughter glow
Across his grave,
And bade the tides above it flow,
Wave hurtling wave,

Shall he not win from latter days
More than his own could yield of praise?
Ay, could the sovereign singer's bays
Forsake his brow,
The warrior's, won on stormier ways,
Still clasp it now.

He loved, and sang of love: he laughed,
And bade the cup whereout he quaffed
Shine as a planet, fore and aft,
And left and right,
And keen as shoots the sun's first shaft
Against the night.

But love and wine were moon and sun
For many a fame long since undone,
And sorrow and joy have lost and won
By stormy turns
As many a singer's soul, if none
More bright than Burns.

And sweeter far in grief or mirth
Have songs as glad and sad of birth
Found voice to speak of wealth or dearth
In joy of life:
But never song took fire from earth
More strong for strife.

The daisy by his ploughshare cleft,
The lips of women loved and left,
The griefs and joys that weave the weft
Of human time,
With craftsman's cunning, keen and deft,
He carved in rhyme.

But Chaucer's daisy shines a star

Above his ploughshare's reach to mar,
And mightier vision gave Dunbar
More strenuous wing
To hear around all sins that are
Hell dance and sing.

And when such pride and power of trust
In song's high gift to arouse from dust
Death, and transfigure love or lust
Through smiles or tears
In golden speech that takes no rust
From cankering years,

As never spake but once in one
Strong star-crossed child of earth and sun,
Villon, made music such as none
May praise or blame,
A crown of starrier flower was won
Than Burns may claim.

But never, since bright earth was born
In rapture of the enkindling morn,
Might godlike wrath and sunlike scorn
That was and is
And shall be while false weeds are worn
Find word like his.

Above the rude and radiant earth
That heaves and glows from firth to firth
In vale and mountain, bright in dearth
And warm in wealth,
Which gave his fiery glory birth
By chance and stealth,

Above the storms of praise and blame
That blur with mist his lustrous name,
His thunderous laughter went and came,
And lives and flies;
The roar that follows on the flame
When lightning dies.

Earth, and the snow-dimmed heights of air,
And water winding soft and fair
Through still sweet places, bright and bare,
By bent and byre,
Taught him what hearts within them were:
But his was fire.

THE COMMONWEAL

A SONG FOR UNIONISTS

Men, whose fathers braved the world in arms against our isles in union,
Men, whose brothers met rebellion face to face,
Show the hearts ye have, if worthy long descent and high communion,
Show the spirits, if unbroken, of your race.

What are these that howl and hiss across the strait of westward water?
What is he who floods our ears with speech in flood?
See the long tongue lick the dripping hand that smokes and reeks of slaughter!
See the man of words embrace the man of blood!

Hear the plea whereby the tonguester mocks and charms the gazing gaper—
"We are they whose works are works of love and peace;
Till disunion bring forth union, what is union, sirs, but paper?
Break and rend it, then shall trust and strength increase."

Who would fear to trust a double-faced but single-hearted dreamer,
Pure of purpose, clean of hand, and clear of guile?
"Life is well-nigh spent," he sighs; "you call me shuffler, trickster, schemer?
I am old—when young men yell at me, I smile."

Many a year that priceless light of life has trembled, we remember,
On the platform of extinction—unextinct;
Many a month has been for him the long year's last—life's calm December:
Can it be that he who said so, saying so, winked?

No; the lust of life, the thirst for work and days with work to do in,
Drove and drives him down the road of splendid shame;
All is well, if o'er the monument recording England's ruin
Time shall read, inscribed in triumph, Gladstone's name.

Thieves and murderers, hands yet red with blood and tongues yet black with lies,
Clap and clamour—"Parnell spurs his Gladstone well!"
Truth, unscared and undeluded by their praise or blame, replies—
"Is the goal of fraud and bloodshed heaven or hell?"

Old men eloquent, who truckle to the traitors of the time,
Love not office—power is no desire of theirs:
What if yesterday their hearts recoiled from blood and fraud and crime?
Conscience erred—an error which to-day repairs.

Conscience only now convinces them of strange though transient error:
Only now they see how fair is treason's face;

See how true the falsehood, just the theft, and blameless is the terror,
Which replaces just and blameless men in place.

Place and time decide the right and wrong of thought and word and action;
Crime is black as hell, till virtue gain its vote;
Then—but ah, to think or say so smacks of fraud or smells of faction!—
Mercy holds the door while Murder hacks the throat.

Murder? Treason? Theft? Poor brothers who succumb to such temptations,
Shall we lay on you or take on us the blame?
Reason answers, and religion echoes round to wondering nations,
"Not with Ireland, but with England rests the shame."

Reason speaks through mild religion's organ, loud and long and lusty—
Profit speaks through lips of patriots pure and true—
"English friends, whose trust we ask for, has not England found us trusty?
Not for us we seek advancement, but for you.

"Far and near the world bears witness of our wisdom, courage, honour;
Egypt knows if there our fame burns bright or dim.
Let but England trust as Gordon trusted, soon shall come upon her
Such deliverance as our daring brought on him.

"Far and wide the world rings record of our faith, our constant dealing,
Love of country, truth to friends, contempt for foes.
Sign once more the bond of trust in us that here awaits but sealing,
We will give yet more than all our record shows.

"Perfect ruin, shame eternal, everlasting degradation,
Freedom bought and sold, truth bound and treason free."
Yet an hour is here for answer; now, if here be yet a nation,
Answer, England, man by man from sea to sea!

June 30, 1886.

THE QUESTION

1887

Shall England consummate the crime
That binds the murderer's hand, and leaves
No surety for the trust of thieves?
Time pleads against it—truth and time—
And pity frowns and grieves.

The hoary henchman of the gang

Lifts hands that never dew nor rain
May cleanse from Gordon's blood again,
Appealing: pity's tenderest pang
Thrills his pure heart with pain.

Grand helmsman of the clamorous crew,
The good grey recreant quakes and weeps
To think that crime no longer creeps
Safe toward its end: that murderers too
May die when mercy sleeps.

While all the lives were innocent
That slaughter drank, and laughed with rage,
Bland virtue sighed, "A former age
Taught murder: souls long discontent
Can aught save blood assuage?

"You blame not Russian hands that smite
By fierce and secret ways the power
That leaves not life one chainless hour;
Have these than they less natural right
To claim life's natural dower?

"The dower that freedom brings the slave
She weds, is vengeance: why should we,
Whom equal laws acclaim as free,
Think shame, if men too blindly brave
Steal, murder, skulk, and flee?

"At kings they strike in Russia: there
Men take their life in hand who slay
Kings: these, that have not heart to lay
Hand save on girls whose ravaged hair
Is made the patriot's prey,

"These, whom the sight of old men slain
Makes bold to bid their children die,
Starved, if they hold not peace, nor lie,
Claim loftier praise: could others deign
To stand in shame so high?

"Could others deign to dare such deeds
As holiest Ireland hallows? Nay,
But justice then makes plain our way:
Be laws burnt up like burning weeds
That vex the face of day.

"Shall bloodmongers be held of us

Blood-guilty? Hands reached out for gold
Whereon blood rusts not yet, we hold
Bloodless and blameless: ever thus
Have good men held of old.

"Fair Freedom, fledged and imped with lies,
Takes flight by night where murder lurks,
And broods on murderous ways and works,
Yet seems not hideous in our eyes
As Austrians or as Turks.

"Be it ours to undo a woful past,
To bid the bells of concord chime,
To break the bonds of suffering crime,
Slack now, that some would make more fast:
Such teaching comes of time."

So pleads the gentlest heart that lives,
Whose pity, pitiless for all
Whom darkling terror holds in thrall,
Toward none save miscreants yearns, and gives
Alms of warm tears—and gall.

Hear, England, and obey: for he
Who claims thy trust again to-day
Is he who left thy sons a prey
To shame whence only death sets free:
Hear, England, and obey.

Thy spoils he gave to deck the Dutch;
Thy noblest pride, most pure, most brave,
To death forlorn and sure he gave;
Nor now requires he overmuch
Who bids thee dig thy grave.

Dig deep the grave of shame, wherein
Thy fame, thy commonweal, must lie;
Put thought of aught save terror by;
To strike and slay the slayer is sin;
And Murder must not die.

Bind fast the true man; loose the thief;
Shamed were the land, the laws accursed,
Were guilt, not innocence, amerced;
And dark the wrong and sore the grief,
Were tyrants too coerced.

The fiercest cowards that ever skulked,

The cowardliest hounds that ever lapped
Blood, if their horde be tracked and trapped,
And justice claim their lives for mulct,
Gnash teeth that flashed and snapped.

Bow down for fear, then, England: bow,
Lest worse befall thee yet; and swear
That nought save pity, conscience, care
For truth and mercy, moves thee now
To call foul falsehood fair.

So shalt thou live in shame, and hear
The lips of all men laugh thee dead;
The wide world's mockery round thy head
Shriek like a storm-wind: and a bier
Shall be thine honour's bed.

APOSTASY

Et Judas m'a dit: Traître!—VICTOR HUGO

I

Truths change with time, and terms with truth. To-day
A statesman worships union, and to-night
Disunion. Shame to have sinned against the light
Confounds not but impels his tongue to unsay
What yestereve he swore. Should fear make way
For treason? honour change her livery? fright
Clasp hands with interest? wrong pledge faith with right?
Religion, mercy, conscience, answer—Yea.

To veer is not to veer: when votes are weighed,
The numerous tongue approves him renegade
Who cannot change his banner: he that can
Sits crowned with wreaths of praise too pure to fade.
Truth smiles applause on treason's poisonous plan:
And Cleon is an honourable man.

II

Pure faith, fond hope, sweet love, with God for guide,
Move now the men whose blameless error cast
In prison (ah, but love condones the past!)
Their subject knaves that were—their lords that ride

Now laughing on their necks, and now bestride
Their vassal backs in triumph. Faith stands fast
Though fear haul down the flag that crowned her mast
And hope and love proclaim that truth has lied.

Turn, turn, and turn—so bids the still small voice,
The changeless voice of honour. He that stands
Where all his life he stood, with bribeless hands,
With tongue unhired to mourn, reprove, rejoice,
Curse, bless, forswear, and swear again, and lie,
Stands proven apostate in the apostate's eye.

III

Fraud shrinks from faith: at sight of swans, the raven
Chides blackness, and the snake recoils aghast
In fear of poison when a bird flies past.
Thersites brands Achilles as a craven;
The shoal fed full with shipwreck blames the haven
For murderous lust of lives devoured, and vast
Desire of doom whose feast is mercy's fast:
And Bacon sees the traitor's mark engraven
Full on the front of Essex. Grief and shame
Obscure the chaste and sunlike spirit of Oates
At thought of Russell's treason; and the name
Of Milton sickens with superb disgust
The heaving heart of Waller. Wisdom dotes,
If wisdom turns not tail and licks not dust.

IV

The sole sweet land found fit to wed the sea,
With reptile rebels at her heel of old,
Set hard her heel upon them, and controlled
The cowering poisonous peril. How should she
Cower, and resign her trust of empire? Free
As winds and waters live the loyal-souled
And true-born sons that love her: nay, the bold
Base knaves who curse her name have leave to be
The loud-tongued liars they are. For she, beyond
All woful years that bid men's hearts despond,
Sees yet the likeness of her ancient fame
Burn from the heavenward heights of history, hears
Not Leicester's name but Sidney's—faith's, not fear's—
Not Gladstone's now but only Gordon's name.

RUSSIA: AN ODE

1890

I

Out of hell a word comes hissing, dark as doom,
Fierce as fire, and foul as plague-polluted gloom;
Out of hell wherein the sinless damned endure
More than ever sin conceived of pains impure;
More than ever ground men's living souls to dust;
Worse than madness ever dreamed of murderous lust.
Since the world's wail first went up from lands and seas
Ears have heard not, tongues have told not things like these.
Dante, led by love's and hate's accordant spell
Down the deepest and the loathliest ways of hell,
Where beyond the brook of blood the rain was fire,
Where the scalps were masked with dung more deep than mire,
Saw not, where the filth was foulest, and the night
Darkest, depths whose fiends could match the Muscovite.
Set beside this truth, his deadliest vision seems
Pale and pure and painless as a virgin's dreams.
Maidens dead beneath the clasping lash, and wives
Rent with deadlier pangs than death—for shame survives,
Naked, mad, starved, scourged, spurned, frozen, fallen, deflowered,
Souls and bodies as by fangs of beasts devoured,
Sounds that hell would hear not, sights no thought could shape,
Limbs that feel as flame the ravenous grasp of rape,
Filth of raging crime and shame that crime enjoys,
Age made one with youth in torture, girls with boys,
These, and worse if aught be worse than these things are,
Prove thee regent, Russia—praise thy mercy, Czar.

II

Sons of man, men born of women, may we dare
Say they sin who dare be slain and dare not spare?
They who take their lives in hand and smile on death,
Holding life as less than sleep's most fitful breath,
So their life perchance or death may serve and speed
Faith and hope, that die if dream become not deed?
Nought is death and nought is life and nought is fate
Save for souls that love has clothed with fire of hate.
These behold them, weigh them, prove them, find them nought,
Save by light of hope and fire of burning thought.

What though sun be less than storm where these aspire,
Dawn than lightning, song than thunder, light than fire?
Help is none in heaven: hope sees no gentler star:
Earth is hell, and hell bows down before the Czar.
All its monstrous, murderous, lecherous births acclaim
Him whose empire lives to match its fiery fame.
Nay, perchance at sight or sense of deeds here done,
Here where men may lift up eyes to greet the sun,
Hell recoils heart-stricken: horror worse than hell
Darkens earth and sickens heaven; life knows the spell,
Shudders, quails, and sinks—or, filled with fierier breath,
Rises red in arms devised of darkling death.
Pity mad with passion, anguish mad with shame,
Call aloud on justice by her darker name;
Love grows hate for love's sake; life takes death for guide.
Night hath none but one red star—Tyrannicide.

III

"God or man, be swift; hope sickens with delay:
Smite, and send him howling down his father's way!
Fall, O fire of heaven, and smite as fire from hell
Halls wherein men's torturers, crowned and cowering, dwell!
These that crouch and shrink and shudder, girt with power—
These that reign, and dare not trust one trembling hour—
These omnipotent, whom terror curbs and drives—
These whose life reflects in fear their victims' lives—
These whose breath sheds poison worse than plague's thick breath—
These whose reign is ruin, these whose word is death,
These whose will turns heaven to hell, and day to night,
These, if God's hand smite not, how shall man's not smite?"
So from hearts by horror withered as by fire
Surge the strains of unappeasable desire;
Sounds that bid the darkness lighten, lit for death;
Bid the lips whose breath was doom yield up their breath;
Down the way of Czars, awhile in vain deferred,
Bid the Second Alexander light the Third.
How for shame shall men rebuke them? how may we
Blame, whose fathers died, and slew, to leave us free?
We, though all the world cry out upon them, know,
Were our strife as theirs, we could not strike but so;
Could not cower, and could not kiss the hands that smite;
Could not meet them armed in sunlit battle's light.
Dark as fear and red as hate though morning rise,
Life it is that conquers; death it is that dies.

FOR GREECE AND CRETE

Storm and shame and fraud and darkness fill the nations full with night:
Hope and fear whose eyes yearn eastward have but fire and sword in sight:
One alone, whose name is one with glory, sees and seeks the light.

Hellas, mother of the spirit, sole supreme in war and peace,
Land of light, whose word remembered bids all fear and sorrow cease,
Lives again, while freedom lightens eastward yet for sons of Greece.

Greece, where only men whose manhood was as godhead ever trod,
Bears the blind world witness yet of light wherewith her feet are shod:
Freedom, armed of Greece was always very man and very God.

Now the winds of old that filled her sails with triumph, when the fleet
Bound for death from Asia fled before them stricken, wake to greet
Ships full-winged again for freedom toward the sacred shores of Crete.

There was God born man, the song that spake of old time said: and there
Man, made even as God by trust that shows him nought too dire to dare,
Now may light again the beacon lit when those we worship were.

Sharp the concert wrought of discord shrills the tune of shame and death,
Turk by Christian fenced and fostered, Mecca backed by Nazareth:
All the powerless powers, tongue-valiant, breathe but greed's or terror's breath.

Though the tide that feels the west wind lift it wave by widening wave
Wax not yet to height and fullness of the storm that smites to save,
None shall bid the flood back seaward till no bar be left to brave.

DELPHIC HYMN TO APOLLO

(B.C. 280)

DONE INTO ENGLISH

I

Thee, the son of God most high,
Famed for harping song, will I
Proclaim, and the deathless oracular word
From the snow-topped rock that we gaze on heard,
Counsels of thy glorious giving
Manifest for all men living,
How thou madest the tripod of prophecy thine

Which the wrath of the dragon kept guard on, a shrine
Voiceless till thy shafts could smite
All his live coiled glittering might.

II

Ye that hold of right alone
All deep woods on Helicon,
Fair daughters of thunder-girt God, with your bright
White arms uplift as to lighten the light,
Come to chant your brother's praise,
Gold-haired Phoebus, loud in lays,
Even his, who afar up the twin-topped seat
Of the rock Parnassian whereon we meet
Risen with glorious Delphic maids
Seeks the soft spring-sweetened shades
Castalian, fain of the Delphian peak
Prophetic, sublime as the feet that seek.
Glorious Athens, highest of state,
Come, with praise and prayer elate,
O thou that art queen of the plain unscarred
That the warrior Tritonid hath alway in guard,
Where on many a sacred shrine
Young bulls' thigh-bones burn and shine
As the god that is fire overtakes them, and fast
The smoke of Arabia to heavenward is cast,
Scattering wide its balm: and shrill
Now with nimble notes that thrill
The flute strikes up for the song, and the harp of gold
Strikes up to the song sweet answer: and all behold,
All, aswarm as bees, give ear,
Who by birth hold Athens dear.

A NEW CENTURY

An age too great for thought of ours to scan,
A wave upon the sleepless sea of time
That sinks and sleeps for ever, ere the chime
Pass that salutes with blessing, not with ban,
The dark year dead, the bright year born for man,
Dies: all its days that watched man cower and climb,
Frail as the foam, and as the sun sublime,
Sleep sound as they that slept ere these began.

Our mother earth, whose ages none may tell,

Puts on no change: time bids not her wax pale
Or kindle, quenched or quickened, when the knell
Sounds, and we cry across the veering gale
Farewell—and midnight answers us, Farewell;
Hail—and the heaven of morning answers, Hail.

SEPTEMBER 1896

WRITTEN ON THE NEWS OF THE DEATH OF LORD LEIGHTON

A light has passed that never shall pass away,
A sun has set whose rays are unquelled of night.
The loyal grace, the courtesy bright as day,
The strong sweet radiant spirit of life and light
That shone and smiled and lightened on all men's sight,
The kindly life whose tune was the tune of May,
For us now dark, for love and for fame is bright.

Nay, not for us that live as the fen-fires live,
As stars that shoot and shudder with life and die,
Can death make dark that lustre of life, or give
The grievous gift of trust in oblivion's lie.
Days dear and far death touches, and draws them nigh,
And bids the grief that broods on their graves forgive
The day that seems to mock them as clouds that fly.

If life be life more faithful than shines on sleep
When dreams take wing and lighten and fade like flame,
Then haply death may be not a death so deep
That all things past are past for it wholly—fame,
Love, loving-kindness, seasons that went and came,
And left their light on life as a seal to keep
Winged memory fast and heedful of time's dead claim.

Death gives back life and light to the sunless years
Whose suns long sunken set not for ever. Time,
Blind, fierce, and deaf as tempest, relents, and hears
And sees how bright the days and how sweet their chime
Rang, shone, and passed in music that matched the clime
Wherein we met rejoicing—a joy that cheers
Sorrow, to see the night as the dawn sublime.

The days that were outlighten the days that are,
And eyes now darkened shine as the stars we see

And hear not sing, impassionate star to star,
As once we heard the music that haply he
Hears, high in heaven if ever a voice may be
The same in heaven, the same as on earth, afar
From pain and earth as heaven from the heaving sea.

A woman's voice, divine as a bird's by dawn
Kindled and stirred to sunward, arose and held
Our souls that heard, from earth as from sleep withdrawn,
And filled with light as stars, and as stars compelled
To move by might of music, elate while quelled,
Subdued by rapture, lit as a mountain lawn
By morning whence all heaven in the sunrise welled.

And her the shadow of death as a robe clasped round
Then: and as morning's music she passed away.
And he then with us, warrior and wanderer, crowned
With fame that shone from eastern on western day,
More strong, more kind, than praise or than grief might say,
Has passed now forth of shadow by sunlight bound,
Of night shot through with light that is frail as May.

May dies, and light grows darkness, and life grows death:
Hope fades and shrinks and falls as a changing leaf:
Remembrance, touched and kindled by love's live breath,
Shines, and subdues the shadow of time called grief,
The shade whose length of life is as life's date brief,
With joy that broods on the sunlight past, and saith
That thought and love hold sorrow and change in fief.

Sweet, glad, bright spirit, kind as the sun seems kind
When earth and sea rejoice in his gentler spell,
Thy face that was we see not; bereft and blind,
We see but yet, rejoicing to see, and dwell
Awhile in days that heard not the death-day's knell,
A light so bright that scarcely may sorrow find
One old sweet word that hails thee and mourns—Farewell.

TO GEORGE FREDERICK WATTS

ON THE EIGHTIETH ANNIVERSARY OF HIS BIRTH, FEBRUARY 23, 1897

High thought and hallowed love, by faith made one,
Begat and bare the sweet strong-hearted child,
Art, nursed of Nature; earth and sea and sun
Saw Nature then more godlike as she smiled.

Life smiled on death, and death on life: the Soul
Between them shone, and soared above their strife,
And left on Time's unclosed and starry scroll
A sign that quickened death to deathless life.
Peace rose like Hope, a patient queen, and bade
Hell's firstborn, Faith, abjure her creed and die;
And Love, by life and death made sad and glad,
Gave Conscience ease, and watched Good Will pass by.
All these make music now of one man's name,
Whose life and age are one with love and fame.

ON THE DEATH OF MRS. LYNN LINTON

Kind, wise, and true as truth's own heart,
A soul that here
Chose and held fast the better part
And cast out fear,

Has left us ere we dreamed of death
For life so strong,
Clear as the sundawn's light and breath,
And sweet as song.

We see no more what here awhile
Shed light on men:
Has Landor seen that brave bright smile
Alive again?

If death and life and love be one
And hope no lie
And night no stronger than the sun,
These cannot die.

The father-spirit whence her soul
Took strength, and gave
Back love, is perfect yet and whole,
As hope might crave.

His word is living light and fire:
And hers shall live
By grace of all good gifts the sire
Gave power to give.

The sire and daughter, twain and one
In quest and goal,
Stand face to face beyond the sun,

And soul to soul.

Not we, who loved them well, may dream
What joy sublime
Is theirs, if dawn through darkness gleam,
And life through time.

Time seems but here the mask of death,
That falls and shows
A void where hope may draw not breath:
Night only knows.

Love knows not: all that love may keep
Glad memory gives:
The spirit of the days that sleep
Still wakes and lives.

But not the spirit's self, though song
Would lend it speech,
May touch the goal that hope might long
In vain to reach.

How dear that high true heart, how sweet
Those keen kind eyes,
Love knows, who knows how fiery fleet
Is life that flies.

If life there be that flies not, fair
The life must be
That thrills her sovereign spirit there
And sets it free.

IN MEMORY OF AURELIO SAFFI

Beloved above all nations, land adored,
Sovereign in spirit and charm, by song and sword,
Sovereign whose life is love, whose name is light,
Italia, queen that hast the sun for lord,

Bride that hast heaven for bridegroom, how should night
Veil or withhold from faith's and memory's sight
A man beloved and crowned of thee and fame,
Hide for an hour his name's memorial might?

Thy sons may never speak or hear the name
Saffi, and feel not love's regenerate flame

Thrill all the quickening heart with faith and pride
In one whose life makes death and life the same.

They die indeed whose souls before them died:
Not he, for whom death flung life's portal wide,
Who stands where Dante's soul in vision came,
In Dante's presence, by Mazzini's side.

March 26, 1896.

CARNOT

Death, winged with fire of hate from deathless hell
Wherein the souls of anarchs hiss and die,
With stroke as dire has cloven a heart as high
As twice beyond the wide sea's westward swell
The living lust of death had power to quell
Through ministry of murderous hands whereby
Dark fate bade Lincoln's head and Garfield's lie
Low even as his who bids his France farewell.

France, now no heart that would not weep with thee
Loved ever faith or freedom. From thy hand
The staff of state is broken: hope, unmanned
With anguish, doubts if freedom's self be free.
The snake-souled anarch's fang strikes all the land
Cold, and all hearts unsundered by the sea.

June 25, 1894.

AFTER THE VERDICT

France, cloven in twain by fire of hell and hate,
Shamed with the shame of men her meanest born,
Soldier and judge whose names, inscribed for scorn,
Stand vilest on the record writ of fate,
Lies yet not wholly vile who stood so great,
Sees yet not all her praise of old outworn.
Not yet is all her scroll of glory torn,
Or left for utter shame to desecrate.
High souls and constant hearts of faithful men
Sustain her perfect praise with tongue and pen
Indomitable as honour. Storms may toss
And soil her standard ere her bark win home:

But shame falls full upon the Christless cross
Whose brandmark signs the holy hounds of Rome.

September 1899.

THE TRANSVAAL

Patience, long sick to death, is dead. Too long
Have sloth and doubt and treason bidden us be
What Cromwell's England was not, when the sea
To him bore witness given of Blake how strong
She stood, a commonweal that brooked no wrong
From foes less vile than men like wolves set free
Whose war is waged where none may fight or flee—
With women and with weanlings. Speech and song
Lack utterance now for loathing. Scarce we hear
Foul tongues that blacken God's dishonoured name
With prayers turned curses and with praise found shame
Defy the truth whose witness now draws near
To scourge these dogs, agape with jaws afoam,
Down out of life. Strike, England, and strike home.

October 9, 1899.

REVERSE

The wave that breaks against a forward stroke
Beats not the swimmer back, but thrills him through
With joyous trust to win his way anew
Through stronger seas than first upon him broke
And triumphed. England's iron-tempered oak
Shrank not when Europe's might against her grew
Full, and her sun drank up her foes like dew,
And lion-like from sleep her strength awoke.

As bold in fight as bold in breach of trust
We find our foes, and wonder not to find,
Nor grudge them praise whom honour may not bind;
But loathing more intense than speaks disgust
Heaves England's heart, when scorn is bound to greet
Hunters and hounds whose tongues would lick their feet.

November 1, 1899.

THE TURNING OF THE TIDE

Storm, strong with all the bitter heart of hate,
Smote England, now nineteen dark years ago,
As when the tide's full wrath in seaward flow
Smites and bears back the swimmer. Fraud and fate
Were leagued against her: fear was fain to prate
Of honour in dishonour, pride brought low,
And humbleness whence holiness must grow,
And greatness born of shame to be so great.

The winter day that withered hope and pride
Shines now triumphal on the turning tide
That sets once more our trust in freedom free,
That leaves a ruthless and a truthless foe
And all base hopes that hailed his cause laid low,
And England's name a light on land and sea.

February 27, 1900.

ON THE DEATH OF COLONEL BENSON

Northumberland, so proud and sad to-day,
Weep and rejoice, our mother, whom no son
More glorious than this dead and deathless one
Brought ever fame whereon no time shall prey.
Nor heed we more than he what liars dare say
Of mercy's holiest duties left undone
Toward whelps and dams of murderous foes, whom none
Save we had spared or feared to starve and slay.

Alone as Milton and as Wordsworth found
And hailed their England, when from all around
Howled all the recreant hate of envious knaves,
Sublime she stands: while, stifled in the sound,
Each lie that falls from German boors and slaves
Falls but as filth dropt in the wandering waves.

November 4, 1901.

ASTRÆA VICTRIX

England, elect of time,
By freedom sealed sublime,
And constant as the sun that saw thy dawn
Outshine upon the sea
His own in heaven, to be
A light that night nor day should see withdrawn,
If song may speak not now thy praise,
Fame writes it higher than song may soar or faith may gaze.

Dark months of months beheld
Hope thwarted, crossed, and quelled,
And heard the heartless hounds of hatred bay
Aloud against thee, glad
As now their souls are sad
Who see their hope in hatred pass away
And wither into shame and fear
And shudder down to darkness, loth to see or hear.

Nought now they hear or see
That speaks or shows not thee
Triumphant; not as empires reared of yore,
The imperial commonweal
That bears thy sovereign seal
And signs thine orient as thy natural shore
Free, as no sons but thine may stand,
Steers lifeward ever, guided of thy pilot hand.

Fear, masked and veiled by fraud,
Found shameful time to applaud
Shame, and bow down thy banner towards the dust,
And call on godly shame
To desecrate thy name
And bid false penitence abjure thy trust:
Till England's heart took thought at last,
And felt her future kindle from her fiery past.

Then sprang the sunbright fire
High as the sun, and higher
Than strange men's eyes might watch it undismayed:
But winds athwart it blew
Storm, and the twilight grew
Darkness awhile, an unenduring shade:
And all base birds and beasts of night
Saw no more England now to fear, no loathsome light.

All knaves and slaves at heart
Who, knowing thee what thou art,
Abhor thee, seeing what none save here may see,

Strong freedom, taintless truth,
Supreme in ageless youth,
Howled all their hate and hope aloud at thee
While yet the wavering wind of strife
Bore hard against her sail whose freight is hope and life.

And now the quickening tide
That brings back power and pride
To faith and love whose ensign is thy name
Bears down the recreant lie
That doomed thy name to die,
Sons, friends, and foes behold thy star the same
As when it stood in heaven a sun
And Europe saw no glory left her sky save one.

And now, as then she saw,
She sees with shamefast awe
How all unlike all slaves and tyrants born
Where bondmen champ the bit
And anarchs foam and flit,
And day mocks day, and year puts year to scorn,
Our mother bore us, English men,
Ashamed of shame and strong in mercy, now as then.

We loosed not on these knaves
Their scourge-tormented slaves:
We held the hand that fain had risen to smite
The torturer fast, and made
Justice awhile afraid,
And righteousness forego her ruthless right:
We warred not even with these as they;
We bade not them they preyed on make of them their prey.

All murderous fraud that lurks
In hearts where hell's craft works
Fought, crawled, and slew in darkness: they that died
Dreamed not of foes too base
For scorn to grant them grace:
Men wounded, women, children at their side,
Had found what faith in fiends may live:
And yet we gave not back what righteous doom would give.

No false white flag that fawns
On faith till murder dawns
Blood-red from hell-black treason's heart of hate
Left ever shame's foul brand
Seared on an English hand:
And yet our pride vouchsafes them grace too great

For other pride to dream of: scorn
Strikes retribution silent as the stars at morn.

And now the living breath
Whose life puts death to death,
Freedom, whose name is England, stirs and thrills
The burning darkness through
Whence fraud and slavery grew,
We scarce may mourn our dead whose fame fulfils
The record where her foes have read
That earth shall see none like her born ere earth be dead.

THE FIRST OF JUNE

Peace and war are one in proof of England's deathless praise.
One divine day saw her foemen scattered on the sea
Far and fast as storm could speed: the same strong day of days
Sees the imperial commonweal set friends and foemen free.
Save where freedom reigns, whose name is England, fraud and fear
Grind and blind the face of men who look on her and lie:
Now may truth and pride in truth, whose seat of old was here,
See them shamed and stricken blind and dumb as worms that die.
Even before our hallowed hawthorn-blossom pass and cease,
Even as England shines and smiles at last upon the sun,
Comes the word that means for England more than passing peace,
Peace with honour, peace with pride in righteous work well done.
Crowned with flowers the first of all the world and all the year,
Peace, whose name is one with honour born of war, is here.

ROUNDEL

FROM THE FRENCH OF VILLON

Death, I would plead against thy wrong,
Who hast reft me of my love, my wife,
And art not satiate yet with strife,
But needs wilt hold me lingering long.
No strength since then has kept me strong:
But what could hurt thee in her life,
Death?

Twain we were, and our hearts one song,
One heart: if that be dead, thy knife
Hath cut me off alive from life,

Dead as the carver's figured throng,
Death!

A ROUNDEL OF RABELAIS

Theleme is afar on the waters, adrift and afar,
Afar and afloat on the waters that flicker and gleam,
And we feel but her fragrance and see but the shadows that mar
Theleme.

In the sun-coloured mists of the sunrise and sunset that steam
As incense from urns of the twilight, her portals ajar
Let pass as a shadow the light of the sound of a dream.

But the laughter that rings from her cloisters that know not a bar
So kindles delight in desire that the souls in us deem
He erred not, the seer who discerned on the seas as a star
Theleme.

LUCIFER

Écrasez l'infâme.—VOLTAIRE

Les prêtres ont raison de l'appeler Lucifer.—VICTOR HUGO

Voltaire, our England's lover, man divine
Beyond all Gods that ever fear adored
By right and might, by sceptre and by sword,
By godlike love of sunlike truth, made thine
Through godlike hate of falsehood's marshlight shine
And all the fume of creeds and deeds abhorred
Whose light was darkness, till the dawn-star soared,
Truth, reason, mercy, justice, keep thy shrine
Sacred in memory's temple, seeing that none
Of all souls born to strive before the sun
Loved ever good or hated evil more.
The snake that felt thy heel upon her head,
Night's first-born, writhes as though she were not dead,
But strikes not, stings not, slays not as before.

THE CENTENARY OF ALEXANDRE DUMAS

Sound of trumpets blowing down the merriest winds of morn,
Flash of hurtless lightnings, laugh of thunders loud and glad,
Here should hail the summer day whereon a light was born
Whence the sun grew brighter, seeing the world less dark and sad.
Man of men by right divine of boyhood everlasting,
France incarnate, France immortal in her deathless boy,
Brighter birthday never shone than thine on earth, forecasting
More of strenuous mirth in manhood, more of manful joy.
Child of warriors, friend of warriors, Garibaldi's friend,
Even thy name is as the splendour of a sunbright sword:
While the boy's heart beats in man, thy fame shall find not end:
Time and dark oblivion bow before thee as their lord.
Youth acclaims thee gladdest of the gods that gild his days:
Age gives thanks for thee, and death lacks heart to quench thy praise.

AT A DOG'S GRAVE

I

Good night, we say, when comes the time to win
The daily death divine that shuts up sight,
Sleep, that assures for all who dwell therein
Good night.

The shadow shed round those we love shines bright
As love's own face, when death, sleep's gentler twin,
From them divides us even as night from light.

Shall friends born lower in life, though pure of sin,
Though clothed with love and faith to usward plight,
Perish and pass unbidden of us, their kin,
Good night?

II

To die a dog's death once was held for shame.
Not all men so beloved and mourned shall lie
As many of these, whose time untimely came
To die.

His years were full: his years were joyous: why
Must love be sorrow, when his gracious name
Recalls his lovely life of limb and eye?

If aught of blameless life on earth may claim

Life higher than death, though death's dark wave rise high,
Such life as this among us never came
To die.

III

White violets, there by hands more sweet than they
Planted, shall sweeten April's flowerful air
About a grave that shows to night and day
White violets there.

A child's light hands, whose touch makes flowers more fair,
Keep fair as these for many a March and May
The light of days that are because they were.

It shall not like a blossom pass away;
It broods and brightens with the days that bear
Fresh fruits of love, but leave, as love might pray,
White violets there.

THREE WEEKS OLD

Three weeks since there was no such rose in being;
Now may eyes made dim with deep delight
See how fair it is, laugh with love, and seeing
Praise the chance that bids us bless the sight.

Three weeks old, and a very rose of roses,
Bright and sweet as love is sweet and bright.
Heaven and earth, till a man's life wanes and closes,
Show not life or love a lovelier sight.

Three weeks past have renewed the rosebright creature
Day by day with life, and night by night.
Love, though fain of its every faultless feature,
Finds not words to match the silent sight.

A CLASP OF HANDS

I

Soft, small, and sweet as sunniest flowers
That bask in heavenly heat

When bud by bud breaks, breathes, and cowers,
Soft, small, and sweet.

A babe's hands open as to greet
The tender touch of ours
And mock with motion faint and fleet

The minutes of the new strange hours
That earth, not heaven, must mete;
Buds fragrant still from heaven's own bowers,
Soft, small, and sweet.

II

A velvet vice with springs of steel
That fasten in a trice
And clench the fingers fast that feel
A velvet vice—

What man would risk the danger twice,
Nor quake from head to heel?
Whom would not one such test suffice?

Well may we tremble as we kneel
In sight of Paradise,
If both a babe's closed fists conceal
A velvet vice.

III

Two flower-soft fists of conquering clutch,
Two creased and dimpled wrists,
That match, if mottled overmuch,
Two flower-soft fists—

What heart of man dare hold the lists
Against such odds and such
Sweet vantage as no strength resists?

Our strength is all a broken crutch,
Our eyes are dim with mists,
Our hearts are prisoners as we touch
Two flower-soft fists.

PROLOGUE TO DOCTOR FAUSTUS

Light, as when dawn takes wing and smites the sea,
Smote England when his day bade Marlowe be.
No fire so keen had thrilled the clouds of time
Since Dante's breath made Italy sublime.
Earth, bright with flowers whose dew shone soft as tears,
Through Chaucer cast her charm on eyes and ears:
The lustrous laughter of the love-lit earth
Rang, leapt, and lightened in his might of mirth.
Deep moonlight, hallowing all the breathless air,
Made earth and heaven for Spenser faint and fair.
But song might bid not heaven and earth be one
Till Marlowe's voice gave warning of the sun.
Thought quailed and fluttered as a wounded bird
Till passion fledged the wing of Marlowe's word.
Faith born of fear bade hope and doubt be dumb
Till Marlowe's pride bade light or darkness come.
Then first our speech was thunder: then our song
Shot lightning through the clouds that wrought us wrong.
Blind fear, whose faith feeds hell with fire, became
A moth self-shrivelled in its own blind flame.
We heard, in tune with even our seas that roll,
The speech of storm, the thunders of the soul.
Men's passions, clothed with all the woes they wrought,
Shone through the fire of man's transfiguring thought.
The thirst of knowledge, quenchless at her springs,
Ambition, fire that clasps the thrones of kings,
Love, light that makes of life one lustrous hour,
And song, the soul's chief crown and throne of power,
The hungering heart of greed and ravenous hate,
Made music high as heaven and deep as fate.
Strange pity, scarce half scornful of her tear,
In Berkeley's vaults bowed down on Edward's bier.
But higher in forceful flight of song than all
The soul of man, its own imperious thrall,
Rose, when his royal spirit of fierce desire
Made life and death for man one flame of fire.
Incarnate man, fast bound as earth and sea,
Spake, when his pride would fain set Faustus free.
Eternal beauty, strong as day and night,
Shone, when his word bade Helen back to sight.
Fear, when he bowed the soul before her spell,
Thundered and lightened through the vaults of hell.
The music known of all men's tongues that sing,
When Marlowe sang, bade love make heaven of spring;
The music none but English tongues may make,
Our own sole song, spake first when Marlowe spake;

And on his grave, though there no stone may stand,
The flower it shows was laid by Shakespeare's hand.

PROLOGUE TO ARDEN OF FEVERSHAM

Love dark as death and fierce as fire on wing
Sustains in sin the soul that feels it cling
Like flame whose tongues are serpents: hope and fear
Die when a love more dire than hate draws near,
And stings to death the heart it cleaves in twain,
And leaves in ashes all but fear and pain.
Our lustrous England rose to life and light
From Rome's and hell's immitigable night,
And music laughed and quickened from her breath,
When first her sons acclaimed Elizabeth.
Her soul became a lyre that all men heard
Who felt their souls give back her lyric word.
Yet now not all at once her perfect power
Spake: man's deep heart abode awhile its hour,
Abode its hour of utterance; not to wake
Till Marlowe's thought in thunderous music spake.
But yet not yet was passion's tragic breath
Thrilled through with sense of instant life and death,
Life actual even as theirs who watched the strife,
Death dark and keen and terrible as life.
Here first was truth in song made perfect: here
Woke first the war of love and hate and fear.
A man too vile for thought's or shame's control
Holds empire on a woman's loftier soul,
And withers it to wickedness: in vain
Shame quickens thought with penitential pain:
In vain dark chance's fitful providence
Withholds the crime, and chills the spirit of sense:
It wakes again in fire that burns away
Repentance, weak as night devoured of day.
Remorse, and ravenous thirst of sin and crime,
Rend and consume the soul in strife sublime,
And passion cries on pity till it hear
And tremble as with love that casts out fear.
Dark as the deed and doom he gave to fame
For ever lies the sovereign singer's name.
Sovereign and regent on the soul he lives
While thought gives thanks for aught remembrance gives,
And mystery sees the imperial shadow stand
By Marlowe's side alone at Shakespeare's hand.

PROLOGUE TO OLD FORTUNATUS

The golden bells of fairyland, that ring
Perpetual chime for childhood's flower-sweet spring,
Sang soft memorial music in his ear
Whose answering music shines about us here.
Soft laughter as of light that stirs the sea
With darkling sense of dawn ere dawn may be,
Kind sorrow, pity touched with gentler scorn,
Keen wit whose shafts were sunshafts of the morn,
Love winged with fancy, fancy thrilled with love,
An eagle's aim and ardour in a dove,
A man's delight and passion in a child,
Inform it as when first they wept and smiled.
Life, soiled and rent and ringed about with pain
Whose touch lent action less of spur than chain,
Left half the happiness his birth designed,
And half the power, unquenched in heart and mind.
Comrade and comforter, sublime in shame,
A poor man bound in prison whence he came
Poor, and took up the burden of his life
Smiling, and strong to strive with sorrow and strife,
He spake in England's ear the poor man's word,
Manful and mournful, deathless and unheard.
His kind great heart was fire, and love's own fire,
Compassion, strong as flesh may feel desire,
To enkindle pity and mercy toward a soul
Sunk down in shame too deep for shame's control.
His kind keen eye was light to lighten hope
Where no man else might see life's darkness ope
And pity's touch bring forth from evil good,
Sweet as forgiveness, strong as fatherhood.
Names higher than his outshine it and outsoar,
But none save one should memory cherish more:
Praise and thanksgiving crown the names above,
But him we give the gift he gave us, love.

PROLOGUE TO THE DUCHESS OF MALFY

When Shakespeare soared from life to death, above
All praise, all adoration, save of love,
As here on earth above all men he stood
That were or are or shall be—great, and good,
Past thank or thought of England or of man—

Light from the sunset quickened as it ran.
His word, who sang as never man may sing
And spake as never voice of man may ring,
Not fruitless fell, as seed on sterile ways,
But brought forth increase even to Shakespeare's praise.
Our skies were thrilled and filled, from sea to sea,
With stars outshining all their suns to be.
No later light of tragic song they knew
Like his whose lightning clove the sunset through.
Half Shakespeare's glory, when his hand sublime
Bade all the change of tragic life and time
Live, and outlive all date of quick and dead,
Fell, rested, and shall rest on Webster's head.
Round him the shadows cast on earth by light
Rose, changed, and shone, transfiguring death and night.
Where evil only crawled and hissed and slew
On ways where nought save shame and bloodshed grew,
He bade the loyal light of honour live,
And love, when stricken through the heart, forgive.
Deep down the midnight of the soul of sin
He lit the star of mercy throned therein.
High up the darkness of sublime despair
He set the sun of love to triumph there.
Things foul or frail his touch made strong and pure,
And bade things transient like to stars endure.
Terror, on wings whose flight made night in heaven,
Pity, with hands whence life took love for leaven,
Breathed round him music whence his mortal breath
Drew life that bade forgetfulness and death
Die: life that bids his light of fiery fame
Endure with England's, yea, with Shakespeare's name.

PROLOGUE TO THE REVENGER'S TRAGEDY

Fire, and behind the breathless flight of fire
Thunder that quickens fear and quells desire,
Make bright and loud the terror of the night
Wherein the soul sees only wrath for light.
Wrath winged by love and sheathed by grief in steel
Sets on the front of crime death's withering seal.
The heaving horror of the storms of sin
Brings forth in fear the lightning hid therein,
And flashes back to darkness: truth, found pure
And perfect, asks not heaven if shame endure.
What life and death were his whose raging song
Bore heaven such witness of the wild world's wrong,

What hand was this that grasped such thunder, none
Knows: night and storm seclude him from the sun.
By daytime none discerns the fire of Mars:
Deep darkness bares to sight the sterner stars,
The lights whose dawn seems doomsday. None may tell
Whence rose a world so lit from heaven and hell.
Life-wasting love, hate born of raging lust,
Fierce retribution, fed with death's own dust
And sorrow's pampering poison, cross and meet,
And wind the world in passion's winding-sheet.
So, when dark faith in faith's dark ages heard
Falsehood, and drank the poison of the Word,
Two shades misshapen came to monstrous birth,
A father fiend in heaven, a thrall on earth:
Man, meanest born of beasts that press the sod,
And die: the vilest of his creatures, God.
A judge unjust, a slave that praised his name,
Made life and death one fire of sin and shame.
And thence reverberate even on Shakespeare's age
A light like darkness crossed his sunbright stage.
Music, sublime as storm or sorrow, sang
Before it: tempest like a harpstring rang.
The fiery shadow of a name unknown
Rose, and in song's high heaven abides alone.

PROLOGUE TO THE BROKEN HEART

The mightiest choir of song that memory hears
Gave England voice for fifty lustrous years.
Sunrise and thunder fired and shook the skies
That saw the sun-god Marlowe's opening eyes.
The morn's own music, answered of the sea,
Spake, when his living lips bade Shakespeare be,
And England, made by Shakespeare's quickening breath
Divine and deathless even till life be death,
Brought forth to time such godlike sons of men
That shamefaced love grows pride, and now seems then.
Shame that their day so shone, so sang, so died,
Remembering, finds remembrance one with pride.
That day was clouding toward a stormlit close
When Ford's red sphere upon the twilight rose.
Sublime with stars and sunset fire, the sky
Glowed as though day, nigh dead, should never die.
Sorrow supreme and strange as chance or doom
Shone, spake, and shuddered through the lustrous gloom.
Tears lit with love made all the darkening air

Bright as though death's dim sunrise thrilled it there
And life re-risen took comfort. Stern and still
As hours and years that change and anguish fill,
The strong secluded spirit, ere it woke,
Dwelt dumb till power possessed it, and it spoke.
Strange, calm, and sure as sense of beast or bird,
Came forth from night the thought that breathed the word;
That chilled and thrilled with passion-stricken breath
Halls where Calantha trod the dance of death.
A strength of soul too passionately pure
To change for aught that horror bids endure,
To quail and wail and weep faint life away
Ere sovereign sorrow smite, relent, and slay,
Sustained her silent, till her bridal bloom
Changed, smiled, and waned in rapture toward the tomb.
Terror twin-born with pity kissed and thrilled
The lips that Shakespeare's word or Webster's filled:
Here both, cast out, fell silent: pity shrank,
Rebuked, and terror, spirit-stricken, sank:
The soul assailed arose afar above
All reach of all but only death and love.

PROLOGUE TO A VERY WOMAN

Swift music made of passion's changeful power,
Sweet as the change that leaves the world in flower
When spring laughs winter down to deathward, rang
From grave and gracious lips that smiled and sang
When Massinger, too wise for kings to hear
And learn of him truth, wisdom, faith, or fear,
Gave all his gentler heart to love's light lore,
That grief might brood and scorn breed wrath no more.
Soft, bright, fierce, tender, fitful, truthful, sweet,
A shrine where faith and change might smile and meet,
A soul whose music could but shift its tune
As when the lustrous year turns May to June
And spring subsides in summer, so makes good
Its perfect claim to very womanhood.
The heart that hate of wrong made fire, the hand
Whose touch was fire as keen as shame's own brand
When fraud and treason, swift to smile and sting,
Crowned and discrowned a tyrant, knave or king,
False each and ravenous as the fitful sea,
Grew gently glad as love that fear sets free.
Like eddying ripples that the wind restrains,
The bright words whisper music ere it wanes.

Ere fades the sovereign sound of song that rang
As though the sun to match the sea's tune sang,
When noon from dawn took life and light, and time
Shone, seeing how Shakespeare made the world sublime,
Ere sinks the wind whose breath was heaven's and day's,
The sunset's witness gives the sundawn praise.

PROLOGUE TO THE SPANISH GIPSY

The wind that brings us from the springtide south
Strange music as from love's or life's own mouth
Blew hither, when the blast of battle ceased
That swept back southward Spanish prince and priest,
A sound more sweet than April's flower-sweet rain,
And bade bright England smile on pardoned Spain.
The land that cast out Philip and his God
Grew gladly subject where Cervantes trod.
Even he whose name above all names on earth
Crowns England queen by grace of Shakespeare's birth
Might scarce have scorned to smile in God's wise down
And gild with praise from heaven an earthlier crown.
And he whose hand bade live down lengthening years
Quixote, a name lit up with smiles and tears,
Gave the glad watchword of the gipsies' life,
Where fear took hope and grief took joy to wife.
Times change, and fame is fitful as the sea:
But sunset bids not darkness always be,
And still some light from Shakespeare and the sun
Burns back the cloud that masks not Middleton.
With strong swift strokes of love and wrath he drew
Shakespearean London's loud and lusty crew:
No plainer might the likeness rise and stand
When Hogarth took his living world in hand.
No surer then his fire-fledged shafts could hit,
Winged with as forceful and as faithful wit:
No truer a tragic depth and heat of heart
Glowed through the painter's than the poet's art.
He lit and hung in heaven the wan fierce moon
Whose glance kept time with witchcraft's air-struck tune:
He watched the doors where loveless love let in
The pageant hailed and crowned by death and sin:
He bared the souls where love, twin-born with hate,
Made wide the way for passion-fostered fate.
All English-hearted, all his heart arose
To scourge with scorn his England's cowering foes:
And Rome and Spain, who bade their scorner be

Their prisoner, left his heart as England's free.
Now give we all we may of all his due
To one long since thus tried and found thus true.

PROLOGUE TO THE TWO NOBLE KINSMEN

Sweet as the dewfall, splendid as the south,
Love touched with speech Boccaccio's golden mouth,
Joy thrilled and filled its utterance full with song,
And sorrow smiled on doom that wrought no wrong.
A starrier lustre of lordlier music rose
Beyond the sundering bar of seas and snows
When Chaucer's thought took life and light from his
And England's crown was one with Italy's.
Loftiest and last, by grace of Shakespeare's word,
Arose above their quiring spheres a third,
Arose, and flashed, and faltered: song's deep sky
Saw Shakespeare pass in light, in music die.
No light like his, no music, man might give
To bid the darkened sphere, left songless, live.
Soft though the sound of Fletcher's rose and rang
And lit the lunar darkness as it sang,
Below the singing stars the cloud-crossed moon
Gave back the sunken sun's a trembling tune.
As when at highest high tide the sovereign sea
Pauses, and patience doubts if passion be,
Till gradual ripples ebb, recede, recoil,
Shine, smile, and whisper, laughing as they toil,
Stark silence fell, at turn of fate's high tide,
Upon his broken song when Shakespeare died,
Till Fletcher's light sweet speech took heart to say
What evening, should it speak for morning, may.
And fourfold now the gradual glory shines
That shows once more in heaven two twinborn signs,
Two brethren stars whose light no cloud may fret,
No soul whereon their story dawns forget.

THE AFTERGLOW OF SHAKESPEARE

Let there be light, said Time: and England heard:
And manhood grew to godhead at the word.
No light had shone, since earth arose from sleep,
So far; no fire of thought had cloven so deep.
A day beyond all days bade life acclaim

Shakespeare: and man put on his crowning name.
All secrets once through darkling ages kept
Shone, sang, and smiled to think how long they slept.
Man rose past fear of lies whereon he trod:
And Dante's ghost saw hell devour his God.
Bright Marlowe, brave as winds that brave the sea
When sundawn bids their bliss in battle be,
Lit England first along the ways whereon
Song brighter far than sunlight soared and shone.
He died ere half his life had earned his right
To lighten time with song's triumphant light.
Hope shrank, and felt the stroke at heart: but one
She knew not rose, a man to match the sun.
And England's hope and time's and man's became
Joy, deep as music's heart and keen as flame.
Not long, for heaven on earth may live not long,
Light sang, and darkness died before the song.
He passed, the man above all men, whose breath
Transfigured life with speech that lightens death.
He passed: but yet for many a lustrous year
His light of song bade England shine and hear.
As plague and fire and faith in falsehood spread,
So from the man of men, divine and dead,
Contagious godhead, seen, unknown, and heard,
Fulfilled and quickened England; thought and word,
When men would fain set life to music, grew
More sweet than years which knew not Shakespeare knew.
The simplest soul that set itself to song
Sang, and may fear not time's or change's wrong.
The lightest eye that glanced on life could see
Through grief and joy the God that man might be.
All passion whence the living soul takes fire
Till death fulfil despair and quench desire,
All love that lightens through the cloud of chance,
All hate that lurks in hope and smites askance,
All holiness of sorrow, all divine
Pity, whose tears are stars that save and shine,
All sunbright strength of laughter like the sea's
When spring and autumn loose their lustrous breeze,
All sweet, all strange, all sad, all glorious things,
Lived on his lips, and hailed him king of kings.
All thought, all strife, all anguish, all delight,
Spake all he bade, and speak till day be night.
No soul that heard, no spirit that beheld,
Knew not the God that lured them and compelled.
On Beaumont's brow the sun arisen afar
Shed fire which lit through heaven the younger star
That sank before the sunset: one dark spring

Slew first the kinglike subject, then the king.
The glory left above their graves made strong
The heart of Fletcher, till the flower-sweet song
That Shakespeare culled from Chaucer's field, and died,
Found ending on his lips that smiled and sighed.
From Dekker's eyes the light of tear-touched mirth
Shone as from Shakespeare's, mingling heaven and earth.
Wild witchcraft's lure and England's love made one
With Shakespeare's heart the heart of Middleton.
Harsh, homely, true, and tragic, Rowley told
His heart's debt down in rough and radiant gold.
The skies that Tourneur's lightning clove and rent
Flamed through the clouds where Shakespeare's thunder went.
Wise Massinger bade kings be wise in vain
Ere war bade song, storm-stricken, cower and wane.
Kind Heywood, simple-souled and single-eyed,
Found voice for England's home-born praise and pride.
Strange grief, strange love, strange terror, bared the sword
That smote the soul by grace and will of Ford.
The stern grim strength of Chapman's thought found speech
Loud as when storm at ebb-tide rends the beach:
And all the honey brewed from flowers in May
Made sweet the lips and bright the dreams of Day.
But even as Shakespeare caught from Marlowe's word
Fire, so from his the thunder-bearing third,
Webster, took light and might whence none but he
Hath since made song that sounded so the sea
Whose waves are lives of men—whose tidestream rolls
From year to darkening year the freight of souls.
Alone above it, sweet, supreme, sublime,
Shakespeare attunes the jarring chords of time;
Alone of all whose doom is death and birth,
Shakespeare is lord of souls alive on earth.

CLEOPATRA

"Her beauty might outface the jealous hours,
Turn shame to love and pain to a tender sleep,
And the strong nerve of hate to sloth and tears;
Make spring rebellious in the sides of frost,
Thrust out lank winter with hot August growths,
Compel sweet blood into the husks of death,
And from strange beasts enforce harsh courtesy."

T. HAYMAN, Fall of Antony, 1655.

CLEOPATRA

I

Her mouth is fragrant as a vine,
A vine with birds in all its boughs;
Serpent and scarab for a sign
Between the beauty of her brows
And the amorous deep lids divine.

II

Her great curled hair makes luminous
Her cheeks, her lifted throat and chin
Shall she not have the hearts of us
To shatter, and the loves therein
To shred between her fingers thus?

III

Small ruined broken strays of light,
Pearl after pearl she shreds them through
Her long sweet sleepy fingers, white
As any pearl's heart veined with blue,
And soft as dew on a soft night.

IV

As if the very eyes of love
Shone through her shutting lids, and stole
The slow looks of a snake or dove;
As if her lips absorbed the whole
Of love, her soul the soul thereof.

V

Lost, all the lordly pearls that were
Wrung from the sea's heart, from the green
Coasts of the Indian gulf-river;
Lost, all the loves of the world—so keen
Towards this queen for love of her.

VI

You see against her throat the small
Sharp glittering shadows of them shake;
And through her hair the imperial
Curled likeness of the river snake,
Whose bite shall make an end of all.

VII

Through the scales sheathing him like wings,
Through hieroglyphs of gold and gem,
The strong sense of her beauty stings,
Like a keen pulse of love in them,
A running flame through all his rings.

VIII

Under those low large lids of hers
She hath the histories of all time;
The fruit of foliage-stricken years;
The old seasons with their heavy chime
That leaves its rhyme in the world's ears.

IX

She sees the hand of death made bare,
The ravelled riddle of the skies,
The faces faded that were fair,
The mouths made speechless that were wise,
The hollow eyes and dusty hair;

X

The shape and shadow of mystic things,
Things that fate fashions or forbids;
The staff of time-forgotten Kings
Whose name falls off the Pyramids,
Their coffin-lids and grave-clothings;

XI

Dank dregs, the scum of pool or clod,

God-spawn of lizard-footed clans,
And those dog-headed hulks that trod
Swart necks of the old Egyptians,
Raw draughts of man's beginning God;

XII

The poised hawk, quivering ere he smote,
With plume-like gems on breast and back;
The asps and water-worms afloat
Between the rush-flowers moist and slack;
The cat's warm black bright rising throat.

XIII

The purple days of drouth expand
Like a scroll opened out again;
The molten heaven drier than sand,
The hot red heaven without rain,
Sheds iron pain on the empty land.

XIV

All Egypt aches in the sun's sight;
The lips of men are harsh for drouth,
The fierce air leaves their cheeks burnt white,
Charred by the bitter blowing south,
Whose dusty mouth is sharp to bite.

XV

All this she dreams of, and her eyes
Are wrought after the sense hereof.
There is no heart in her for sighs;
The face of her is more than love—
A name above the Ptolemies.

XVI

Her great grave beauty covers her
As that sleek spoil beneath her feet
Clothed once the anointed soothsayer;
The hallowing is gone forth from it

Now, made unmeet for priests to wear.

XVII

She treads on gods and god-like things,
On fate and fear and life and death,
On hate that cleaves and love that clings,
All that is brought forth of man's breath
And perisheth with what it brings.

XVIII

She holds her future close, her lips
Hold fast the face of things to be;
Actium, and sound of war that dips
Down the blown valleys of the sea,
Far sails that flee, and storms of ships;

XIX

The laughing red sweet mouth of wine
At ending of life's festival;
That spice of cerecloths, and the fine
White bitter dust funereal
Sprinkled on all things for a sign;

XX

His face, who was and was not he,
In whom, alive, her life abode;
The end, when she gained heart to see
Those ways of death wherein she trod,
Goddess by god, with Antony.

DEDICATION

The sea that is life everlasting
And death everlasting as life
Abides not a pilot's forecasting,
Foretells not of peace or of strife.
The might of the night that was hidden
Arises and darkens the day,

A glory rebuked and forbidden,
Time's crown, and his prey.

No sweeter, no kindlier, no fairer,
No lovelier a soul from its birth
Wore ever a brighter and rarer
Life's raiment for life upon earth
Than his who enkindled and cherished
Art's vestal and luminous flame,
That dies not when kingdoms have perished
In storm or in shame.

No braver, no trustier, no purer,
No stronger and clearer a soul
Bore witness more splendid and surer
For manhood found perfect and whole
Since man was a warrior and dreamer
Than his who in hatred of wrong
Would fain have arisen a redeemer
By sword or by song.

Twin brethren in spirit, immortal
As art and as love, which were one
For you from the birthday whose portal
First gave you to sight of the sun,
To-day nor to-night nor to-morrow
May bring you again from above,
Drawn down by the spell of the sorrow
Whose anguish is love.

No light rearising hereafter
Shall lighten us here as of old
When seasons were lustrous as laughter
Of waves that are snowshine and gold.
The dawn that imbues and enkindles
Life's fluctuant and fugitive sea
Dies down as the starshine that dwindles
And cares not to be.

Men, mightier than death which divides us,
Friends, dearer than sorrow can say,
The light that is darkness and hides us
Awhile from each other away
Abides but awhile and endures not,
We know, though the day be as night,
For souls that forgetfulness lures not
Till sleep be in sight.

The sleep that enfolds you, the slumber
Supreme and eternal on earth,
Whence ages of numberless number
Shall bring us not back into birth,
We know not indeed if it be not
What no man hath known if it be,
Life, quickened with light that we see not
If spirits may see.

The love that would see and would know it
Is even as the love of a child.
But the fire of the fame of the poet
Who gazed on the past, and it smiled,
But the light of the fame of the painter
Whose hand was as morning's in May,
Death bids not be darker or fainter,
Time casts not away.

We, left of them loveless and lonely,
Who lived in the light of their love,
Whose darkness desires it, we only,
Who see them afar and above,
So far, if we die not, above us,
So lately no dearer than near,
May know not of death if they love us,
Of night if they hear.

We, stricken and darkling and living,
Who loved them and love them, abide
A day, and the gift of its giving,
An hour, and the turn of its tide,
When twilight and midnight and morrow
Shall pass from the sight of the sun,
And death be forgotten, and sorrow
Discrowned and undone.

For us as for these will the breathless
Brief minute arise and pass by:
And if death be not utterly deathless,
If love do not utterly die,
From the life that is quenched as an ember
The soul that aspires as a flame
Can choose not but wholly remember
Love, lovelier than fame.

Though sure be the seal of their glory
And fairer no fame upon earth,
Though never a leaf shall grow hoary

Of the crowns that were given them at birth,
While time as a vassal doth duty
To names that he towers not above,
More perfect in price and in beauty
For ever is love.

The night is upon us, and anguish
Of longing that yearns for the dead.
But mourners that faint not or languish,
That veil not and bow not the head,
Take comfort to heart if a token
Be given them of comfort to be:
While darkness on earth is unbroken,
Light lives on the sea.

Algernon Charles Swinburne – A Short Biography

Algernon Charles Swinburne was born at 7 Chester Street, Grosvenor Place, in London, on April 5th, 1837. He was the eldest of six children born to Captain Charles Henry Swinburne and Lady Jane Henrietta, daughter of the 3rd Earl of Ashburnham, a wealthy Northumbrian family.

Swinburne spent his early years at East Dene in Bonchurch, on the Isle of Wight. As a child, Swinburne was nervous and frail, but also imbued with a nervous energy and fearlessness almost to the point of recklessness.

He was schooled at Eton College from 1849 to 1853. It was here that he first began to write poetry. He excelled at languages and whilst still at Eton won first prizes in both French and Italian.

From Eton he moved to Oxford where he attended at Balliol College from 1856. Here he met friends to whom he became closely attached, among them Dante Gabriel Rossetti, William Morris and Edward Burne-Jones, who in 1857, were painting their Arthurian murals on the walls of the Oxford Union. At Oxford Swinburne was mentored by Benjamin Jowett, the master of Balliol College, who recognised his poetic talent and, intervening on his behalf, tried to keep him from being expelled when he celebrated the Italian patriot Orsini, and his failed attempt on the life of Napoleon III in 1858. Swinburne had to leave the Universcity for a few months due to this but returned in May, 1860 but never received a degree.

Summers were usually spent at Capheaton Hall in Northumberland, the house of his grandfather, Sir John Swinburne, 6th Baronet, who had a famous library and was himself President of the Literary and Philosophical Society in Newcastle upon Tyne.

Swinburne proudly considered himself a native of Northumberland and this is reflected in poems such as the intensely patriotic 'Northumberland' and 'Grace Darling'. He enjoyed riding across the moors and was, it was said, a daring horseman, as he moved 'through honeyed leagues of the northland border', as he remembered the Scottish border in his Recollections.

In the period from 1857 to 1860, Swinburne was one of a number of Pre-Raphaelite's who visited and became part of Lady Pauline Trevelyan's intellectual circle at Wallington Hall, a few miles west of Morpeth in Northumberland.

After leaving college, he moved to London and began his career in earnest as well as becoming a constant visitor to the Rossetti's house. To Rossetti Swinburne was his 'little Northumbrian friend', an affectionate reference to Swinburne's small stature—a mere five foot four. Whatever Swinburne lacked in height he made up for in poetic talent. However, with the burden of such great talent came the unveiling of a dark side that was to cause him pain and would, at times, threaten his very existence with all manner of self-inflicted pains through drink, drugs and sado-machoism.

In 1860 Swinburne published two verse dramas; The Queen Mother and Rosamond but it would not be until 1865 that Swinburne would achieve literary success with Atalanta in Calydon.

In 1861, Swinburne visited Menton on the French Riviera to recover from the effects of yet another period of excess use of alcohol, staying at the Villa Laurenti. From Menton, Swinburne then travelled on to Italy, where he journeyed widely.

After Elizabeth Rossetti's death from suicide in 1862, he and Rossetti moved to Tudor House at 16 Cheyne Walk in Chelsea. The stories that survive from his year with Rossetti are typical Swinburne. In one, Rossetti once had to tell him to keep down the noise — he and a boyfriend had been sliding naked down the bannisters and disturbing Rossetti's painting. He took a sardonic delight in what the critic and biographer, Cecil Lang, calls "Algernonic exaggeration": When people began to talk scathingly about his homosexuality and other sexual proclivities, he circulated a story that he had engaged in pederasty and bestiality with a monkey — and then eaten it. How many of the stories were true and how many invented is unclear. Oscar Wilde called him "a braggart in matters of vice, who had done everything he could to convince his fellow citizens of his homosexuality and bestiality without being in the slightest degree a homosexual or a bestialiser."

In December 1862, Swinburne accompanied Scott and his guests on a trip to Tynemouth. Scott writes in his memoirs that, as they walked by the sea, Swinburne declaimed the as yet unpublished 'Hymn to Proserpine' and 'Laus Veneris' in his lilting intonation, while the waves 'were running the whole length of the long level sands towards Cullercoats and sounding like far-off acclamations'.

Swinburne possessed a curious combination of frail health and strength. He was small and slightly built, but an excellent swimmer and the first to climb Culver Cliff on the Isle of Wight. He had an extremely excitable disposition: people who met him described him as a "demoniac boy" who would go skipping about the room declaiming poetry at the top of his voice. In this as in many things, moderation was not the standard for him. Excess was. Once or twice he had fits, thought to be epileptic, in public; but he made this condition much worse by drinking past excess to unconsciousness. More than once he was delivered to the door in the small of the night, dead drunk. Throughout the 1860s and '70s he rode an alcoholic cycle of dissolution, collapse, drying out at home in the country, then returning to London where he would begin the cycle all over again.

His mania for masochism, particularly flagellation, most probably started in early childhood at Eton and was encouraged by his later friendships with Richard Monckton Milnes (one of Tennyson's fellow Apostles), who introduced him to the works of the Marquis de Sade, and Richard Burton, the Victorian explorer and adventurer. Swinburne was an alcoholic and algolagniac (a desire for sexual gratification through inflicting pain on oneself or others; sadomasochism). He found life difficult, unfulfilling but still his poetic talents pushed to the fore.

Although Swinburne continued to publish some works in periodicals in 1865 he was granted recognition by both public and critics with Atalanta in Calydon written in the style of a classical Greek tragedy.

There followed "Laus Veneris" and Poems and Ballads (1866), with their sexually charged passages, absolutely decadent for polite Victorian society, which were attacked all the more violently as a result. The poems written in homage of Sappho of Lesbos such as "Anactoria" and "Sapphics" were especially savaged. The volume also contained poems such as "The Leper," "Laus Veneris," and "St Dorothy" which evoke both Swinburne's and a general Victorian fascination with the Middle Ages, and are explicitly mediaeval in style, tone and construction. With its publication came instant notoriety. He was now identified with indecent and decadent themes and the precept of art for art's sake.

Swinburne's meeting in 1867 with his long-time hero Mazzini, the Italian patriot living in England in exile, was the beginning of a poetical journey that now became more serious and more engaged with serious thought, initially leading to the political poems in the volume Songs Before Sunrise.

Also in 1867 he was introduced to Adah Isaacs Menken, the American actress, poet and circus rider, whose main fame seemed to be riding naked on a horse (in fact she wore tight nude coloured clothing) for her performance in the melodrama Mazeppa (itself based on a poem by Lord Byron). Although they had a short affair Adah's quote implies that Swinburne was not ready for a relationship that did not involve some self-sabotage; "I can't make him understand that biting's no use."

In 1879, with Swinburne nearly dead from alcoholism and dissolution, his legal advisor Theodore Watts-Dunton took him in, and was gradually successful in getting him to adapt to a healthier lifestyle. Swinburne lived the rest of his life at Watts-Dunton's house. He saw less and less of his old bohemian friends, who thought him a prisoner at The Pines, but his growing deafness also accounts for some of his decreased sociability. By now Swinburne was 42, and was moving from a young man of rebelliousness to a figure of social respectability. It was said of Watts-Dunton that he saved the man and killed the poet.

It is clear that Swinburne had an addictive personality, and clearly incapable of moderation in his pursuit of any chosen vices. This, of course, would both nourish and perhaps sabotage his poetic career. His poetry follows the somewhat clichéd pattern of early flourish and later decline; indeed some of the fresher pieces in the second and third series of Poems and Ballads (published in 1878 and 1889) were actually written during his days at Oxford. Nevertheless, his last collection, A Channel Passage, has some beautiful poems, including "The Lake of Gaube."

He is best remembered as the supreme technician in metre, with a versatility which exceeds even Tennyson's, but which lacks a corresponding emotional range. His obsessions are not widely enough shared; and if he cannot shock us by the strangeness of his desires nor the shrillness of his anti-theistical exclamations, often what remains is not enough to fully engage with the audience.

Swinburne is considered a poet of the decadent school, although he perhaps professed to more vice than he actually indulged in to advertise his deviance. Common gossip of the time reported that he also had a deep crush on the explorer Sir Richard Francis Burton, despite the fact that Swinburne himself abhorred travel. Fact and fiction are easily absorbed by the other so are difficult to untangle even now.

Many critics consider his mastery of vocabulary, rhyme and metre impressive, although he has also been criticised for his florid style and word choices that only fit the rhyme scheme rather than contributing to the meaning of the piece. A. E. Housman, although a critic, had great praise for his rhyming ability: to Swinburne the sonnet was child's play: the task of providing four rhymes was not hard enough, and he wrote long poems in which each stanza required eight or ten rhymes, and wrote them so that he never seemed to be saying anything for the rhyme's sake.

Throughout his career Swinburne published literary criticism of great worth. His deep knowledge of world literatures contributed to a critical style rich in quotation, allusion, and comparison. He is particularly noted for discerning studies of Elizabethan dramatists and of many English and French poets and novelists. As well he was a noted essayist and wrote two novels.

Swinburne was nominated for the Nobel Prize in Literature every year from 1903 to 1907 and then again in 1909.

H.P. Lovecraft, the master of the dark side and a decent poet himself, considered Swinburne "the only real poet in either England or America after the death of Mr. Edgar Allan Poe."

Swinburne was also responsible for devising a poetic form called the roundel, a variation of the French Rondeau form. In 1883 he published A Century of Roundels with several of the roundels dedicated to Dante's sister, the poet Christina Georgina Rossetti. Swinburne wrote to Edward Burne-Jones in 1883: "I have got a tiny new book of songs or songlets, in one form and all manner of metres ... just coming out, of which Miss Rossetti has accepted the dedication. I hope you and Georgie [his wife Georgiana] will find something to like among a hundred poems of nine lines each, twenty-four of which are about babies or small children".

Opinions of the Roundel poems move between those who find them captivating and brilliant, to others who find them merely clever and contrived. One of them, A Baby's Death, was set to music by the English composer Sir Edward Elgar as the song "Roundel: The little eyes that never knew Light".

After the first Poems and Ballads, Swinburne's later poetry was devoted more to philosophy and politics, including the unification of Italy, particularly in the volume Songs before Sunrise. He did not stop writing love poetry entirely, indeed it was only in 1882 that his great epic-length poem, Tristram of Lyonesse, was published, its contents lyrical rather than shocking. His versification, and especially his rhyming technique, remain of high quality to the end.

Algernon Charles Swinburne died of influenza, at the Pines in London on April 10th, 1909 at the age of 72. He was buried at St. Boniface Church, Bonchurch on the Isle of Wight.

Algernon Charles Swinburne – A Concise Bibliography

Verse Drama
The Queen Mother (1860)
Rosamond (1860)
Chastelard (1865)
Bothwell (1874)

Mary Stuart (1881)
Marino Faliero (1885)
Locrine (1887)
The Sisters (1892)
Rosamund, Queen of the Lombards (1899)

Poetry
Atalanta in Calydon (1865)*
Poems and Ballads (1866)
Songs Before Sunrise (1871)
Songs of Two Nations (1875)
Erechtheus (1876)*
Poems and Ballads, Second Series (1878)
Songs of the Springtides (1880)
Studies in Song (1880)
The Heptalogia, or the Seven against Sense. A Cap with Seven Bells (1880)
Tristram of Lyonesse (1882)
A Dark Month & Other Poems
A Century of Roundels (1883)
A Midsummer Holiday and Other Poems (1884)
Poems and Ballads, Third Series (1889)
Astrophel and Other Poems (1894)
The Tale of Balen (1896)
A Channel Passage and Other Poems (1904)

*Although formally tragedies, Atlanta in Calydon and Erechtheus are traditionally included with his poetry.

Criticism
William Blake: A Critical Essay (1868, new edition 1906)
Under the Microscope (1872)
George Chapman: A Critical Essay (1875)
Essays and Studies (1875)
A Note on Charlotte Brontë (1877)
A Study of Shakespeare (1880)
A Study of Victor Hugo (1886)
A Study of Ben Johnson (1889)
Studies in Prose and Poetry (1894)
The Age of Shakespeare (1908)
Shakespeare (1909)

Major Collections
The Poems of Algernon Charles Swinburne, 6 vols. 1904.
The Tragedies of Algernon Charles Swinburne, 5 vols. 1905.
The Complete Works of Algernon Charles Swinburne, 20 vols. Bonchurch Edition. 1925-7.
The Swinburne Letters, 6 vols. 1959-62.

www.ingramcontent.com/pod-product-compliance
Lightning Source LLC
Chambersburg PA
CBHW060142050426
42448CB00010B/2253